Joe Pauker's

GET LOST!

the cool guide to amsterdam

Get Lost Publishing

April 2003

British Library in Publication Data. A catalogue record for this book is available from the British Library.

ISBN: 90-76499-03-9

For all their help, advice, information, and support, many thanks to...
Aaron, Adam, American Book Center, Amsterdam Call Girls, Anthony, Candy, Carl, Christian & Ann, Clyde, Curt & Nancy, Dave & Dian, Doug, Ellen, George, The Headshop, Hemp Works, Ian, Juanita & Eamon, Klaus, Kokopelli, Leander, Micha & Machteld, Michel, Miguel, Mom, Monica, Mor & Fred, Nue, Pip, Pollinator, Pop, Richard & Elard, Rick, Roland & Tinne, Rosa & Art, Sagarmatha Seeds, Sensi Seed Bank, Shayana Shop, Steve, Susan, Sylvie, Tess & Rene, Third Gear Entertainment, Uln, Victor... and most of all, Lisa.

Editing and research assistance

Lisa Kristensen

Additional research assistance

Aaron Cole

Cover design and book layout

Ellen Pauker

Photos

Joe Pauker

Printed in Amsterdam with vegetable-based inks on 100% post-consumer recycled paper.

NO MORE
BLOOD FOR OIL

Introduction

Congratulations! In a world that's gone increasingly mad, you've made the wise decision to come to Amsterdam: one of the sanest places on earth. *And one of the most fun.*

When I first came here, I was amazed at how open the city was. There were non-commercial, underground scenes happening everywhere, and they weren't, for the most part, elitist. Everything was accessible to everyone. I decided to write about some of the cool places I was hanging around, so I could share the information with my friends. And that's how *The Cool Guide* was born. Nine editions later, I'm still hanging around town and writing about it.

This new edition has been completely revised and updated. And it continues to be an independent, DIY project. We've sold a few ads to help us cover the costs of printing and paper, but *nobody* pays to be included in *Get Lost!*

We haven't been able to get hemp paper for a few years, but we're happy to be using vegetable-based inks. The book is printed on 100% post-consumer recycled paper. It also now has a stitched binding.

I've tried to be very accurate with regard to prices, opening times, phone numbers and so on, but I'm just a goof, and things change (all the time). Feel free to write if you have any news, suggestions, complaints, or spare change.

Be sure to check the Get Lost Publishing website (*www.xs4all.nl/~getlost*) for updates on the places and info included in The *Cool Guide*.

Thanks for buying this edition of *Get Lost!* Have a great trip!

Get Lost!
Box 18521
1001 WB Amsterdam
The Netherlands

www.xs4all.nl/~getlost

Contents

About The Author

Joe Pauker was the illegitimate son of a crack whore and an unnamed Texas politician. When he was still an infant, he was left in a reed basket on the doorstep of the Chelsea Hotel in New York City.

At the age of four he began running errands for the junkie rock-stars who called the hotel their home. It was also here that he met the Black Panthers and became their youngest member. After a gun fight with police forced him to flee the city, Joe set off for California to follow his dream of becoming a skateboarder. Within hours of his arrival in L.A. he was attacked and beaten up by the Z-boys. Broke, uneducated, and desperate, he joined a gang. Two years later he was discharged from the U.S. army. The following decade was spent doing odd jobs: acting in films with Ron Jeremy; playing with Miles Davis on the *Kind of Blue* sessions; inventing the internet. At the time of his death he had just received a full scholarship to Harvard where he was to major in Fuzzy Math and Grecian. He died after choking on an alcohol-soaked pretzel. He is sorely missed.

Places To Sleep

Accommodation is probably going to be the most expensive part of your stay in Amsterdam, especially since, with the introduction of the euro, most hotels have jacked up their prices substantially. Although there's an abundance of luxury hotel rooms, there just aren't enough inexpensive ones for all the budget-minded visitors to the city. It can be a real drag finding a place to stay - especially during the summer - and if you're in town for just a few days you don't want to waste time; so here are a few hints to help you out.

One possibility is to go with a "runner" (someone who has the shitty job of running back and forth between a hotel and the train station). These people work for small hotels or hostels, or for private homes and guest houses. A lot of the runners carry books with photos of the rooms so you can look at what you're going to be offered before trekking over there. The hotels tend to be dives, but I've found a couple of great private places this way. Go with your instincts: if you don't like the person offering you a room, tell them to forget it.

In the summer, a bed in a hostel runs anywhere from about €16 to €39 and a clean double room for less than €80 is a good deal. In the winter (except around holidays) prices can drop considerably, especially on weekdays.

The Amsterdam Tourist Office (a.k.a. the VVV; across the square in front of Central Station and to your left, or in the station on Platform 2) has a room-finding service. They can book you a dorm bed or a hotel room, but the cheap ones go fast, of course. If you use this service you'll have to pay them a €3 per person service charge, and a deposit (which is later deducted from the price of the room). The people who work at the VVV are very nice and sometimes you can get a good deal, but in high season the line-ups are painfully long and slow. Open: mon-sat 8-20; sun 9-17.

Amsterdam Hotel Service (Damrak 7, 520-7000; *www.amsterdam-ts.nl*), just across the street from Central Station, has last-minute special prices on all categories of hotels. They charge a €3 per person booking fee. You prepay 10% of the room cost there, and the other 90% at the hotel. Open: daily 9-21.

The GWK bank (627-2731) at Central Station also offers a room-finding service. There you pay a €4.50 per person fee and the full amount of the hotel in advance. The fact that you can't see the place first is a drawback, but their "same-day" sell-off rates (on all grades of hotels) are sometimes a real bargain, especially off-season. They're open daily from 7 until 22.45.

There are dozens of online hotel booking agents, but lately a few friends of mine have been getting some great deals via *www.bookings.nl* - even on 5-star hotels!

Finally, wherever you stay, and no matter how safe the place seems, never leave your valuables lying around. Keep your important stuff with you or, even better, leave it in a safety-deposit box if your hotel has one.

hostels

Schiphol Airport

www.schiphol.nl

You know, I've slept in a lot of airports around the world, and Schiphol is definitely the best. They have comfortable couches in the departure lounges (that's in the boarding area, not in the rest of the airport) where you can actually lie down when you crash out. This area is only accessible to passengers until midnight, though: if you don't get there before then, it's plastic chairs or the floor. Before you check in, hit the Food Village supermarket (open daily 6-24) on the arrivals level. It's the cheapest place in the airport for food. And if you need to bathe, there are free showers next to the British Airways lounge. (Like the good couches, it's in the boarding area.) Or else go to the Hotel Mercure (604-1339) near gate "F". They offer showers 24-hours a day in a private cabin (including soap, towel, and a hair dryer) for €12.50. As for breakfast, there are often free cheese samples on offer at the duty-free delicatessen. And upstairs, in the Panorama Lounge, they sell a few reasonably-priced snacks. For your intellectual nourishment, the Rijksmuseum has opened a free, permanent exhibition here of ten major paintings from their collection. You wouldn't want to stay here for your whole trip, but if you have an early flight it's a good way to save the cost of a night's lodging. (See Airport, Getting Out of Amsterdam chapter for transportation options.)

Christian Youth Hostels (The Shelter City, The Shelter Jordan)

www.shelter.nl

Only €15.50 to €16.50 for a dorm bed and breakfast makes these two hostels a great deal. But separate rooms for men and women, curfews, sing-alongs in the lounge, and a clean-cut staff that's looking for converts should be enough to persuade you to spend a little more elsewhere. You'll have to find the addresses yourself.

The Flying Pig - Nieuwendijk 100, 420-6822; Vossiusstraat 46-47, 400-4187

www.flyingpig.nl

The guys who run these places are travellers themselves, which explains such things as the free use of kitchens, late-night bars, free internet access, and the absence of curfews. For hanging out, both locations have lounges, and Nieuwendijk has DJs. All rooms have toilets and showers. Prices include a free, basic breakfast. The hostel on Nieuwendijk (Flying Pig Downtown), is very close to Central Station. The rates per person for shared rooms with 4 to 22 beds range from €20 to €26. Couples can save money and have fun by booking an extra wide bunkbed which, depending on the size of the room, runs from €30 to €39 per bed. They also have a girls-only dorm. The other hostel (Flying Pig Palace) is by Vondelpark. They have shared rooms with 4 to 10 beds for €19 to €24 per person, and double bunks from €28.50 to €36 per bed. Prices drop a bit off-season. A €10 cash deposit for sheets and keys is returned when you leave. Both sites are central, but the neighbourhood around Vondelpark is much nicer. To reach the Palace from Central Station take tram 1, 2, 5 or 6 to Leidseplein. Walk to the Marriott Hotel and turn left. The hostel is on the street that runs along the left side of the park. (Map areas D4, B8)

Tourist Inn - Spuistraat 52, 421-5841

www.tourist-inn.nl

There's nothing fancy about this hostel, but it's a bit more spacious and clean than some of the others in the neighbourhood around Central Station. Dorm beds, depending on the season, cost from €20 to €25 per person on weekdays (that's ok), and €30 to €35 on weekends (that's not). They have an elevator for those with screwed up knees, and there's a TV and phone in every room. Breakfast is included. Doubles and triples are also available, but the price is too high for what they're offering. You can take trams 1, 2, 5, 13 or 17 and get off at the first stop. Or just walk from Central Station. (Map area D4)

Bob's Youth Palace - Nieuwezijds Voorburgwal 92, 623-0063

You can usually find this hostel by looking for a bunch of people sitting on the front steps smoking joints and strumming guitars. This is a pretty cool place where a lot of travellers stay, but it's cheap, simple lodging so don't expect more than the basics. It's right in the centre of the city and €17 gets you a dorm bed and breakfast. They also have a women's dorm. Trams 1, 2, 5, 6, 13 or 17 will take you there, or you can walk from Central Station: it's not far. (Map area D4)

International Youth Hostels - Zandpad 5, 589-8996; Kloveniersburgwal 97, 624-6832
www.njhc.org/vondelpark I www.njhc.org/stadsdoelen

These are "official" youth hostels. The one in Vondelpark (Zandpad 5, a great location) has been completely renovated and all their rooms are equipped with a toilet and shower. They offer dorm beds in larger rooms, depending on the season, from €20 to €24, and quad rooms from €24 to €28 per person. Double rooms cost €60 to €76 per room. Members pay €2.50 less. Sheets are included in the price, as is an all-you-can-eat breakfast. There are also restaurants, a bicycle rental service, internet facilities, and a tourist info centre. And I've been assured that, most of the time, groups of kids on field trips will be booked into a different building from the one housing independent travellers. From Central Station take tram 1, 2, 5 or 6 to Leidseplein. Walk to the Marriott Hotel and turn left. The hostel sign is a block ahead of you. The other location is also nice: on a wide canal right in the centre of the city. There are only dorm rooms there, however. Beds cost €18.15 (€2.50 less if you're a member). (Map areas E6, B7)

hotels

Here are a few places with clean, reasonably-priced rooms. In the summer you should really try to arrange your accommodation in advance, or at least before leaving Central Station (see intro to this chapter for details). Expect prices to jump during holiday periods.

Hemp Hotel Amsterdam - Frederiksplein 15, 625-4425
www.hemp-hotel.com

This little pension in the centre of Amsterdam is totally unique. The five small rooms, all decked out in hemp, each have their own theme. Try sleeping on a hemp mattress for a few nights in the Afghani room. Or, if you've always fancied a visit to the Himalayas, book the Indian room. Rates that include a vegetarian breakfast are €33 for a single, €43 for a double, €70 for a twin with private shower. An extra mattress in the room costs an additional €10. Look for a drop of about 10% off-season. Downstairs, the Hemple Temple bar has turned into a popular late-night hangout. You can party there until 3 on weeknights and 4 on Friday and Saturday. They serve hemp snacks, hemp beer, but alas, no more hemp vodka right out of the freezer. Take tram 4 from Central Station to Frederiksplein. Note: as we go to press there's talk of a move - check the *Get Lost!* website for news. (Map area E8)

Hotel Abba - Overtoom 122, 618-3058

www.abbabudgethotel.com

The staff are friendly and helpful at this hotel. An all-you-can-eat breakfast in a sunny room is included in the price. Depending on the season, singles cost from €25 to €37.50. Doubles (some with shower and toilet) range from €40 to €80. They also have rooms for 4 and 5 people that run from €22.50 to €35 per person. All rooms have TVs. There's a nice view from the front (especially from the upper floors), but it can be a bit noisy because of the street. The free safety-deposit boxes in the reception area are a very nice feature: use them! Close to Leidseplein and Vondelpark. Take tram 1 from Central Station to Constantijn Huygensstraat. (Map area A7)

Hotel Princess - Overtoom 80, 612-2947

http://hotelprincess.myweb.nl

This hotel is located at the corner of a busy intersection about a five-minute walk from Leidseplein, and just up the way from the Abba (see above). It's a bit run down, but has some nice touches like reading lights by the bed. Depending on the season, single rooms cost €38 to €43; twins and doubles (you can request a double bed) are €50 to €66; triples are €85 to €90; quads are €100 to €110. Toilets and showers are all shared, but there are TVs in the rooms. Breakfast is included and it's simple, but filling: bread, cheese, ham, cereal, boiled eggs, juice and coffee. The rest of the day, drinks and snacks are available at the reception. Take tram 1 from Central Station to Constantijn Huygensstraat. (Map area B7)

Hotel Crystal - 2e Helmersstraat 6, 618-0521

Brought to you by the same owners as the Princess, Hotel Crystal is also close to Leidseplein, but on a quieter street. They have singles for €50, and doubles without facilities for €70. Doubles with a shower and toilet go for €102. Triples with facilities are €130, and quads with facilities are €150. All rooms have TVs. An all-you-can-eat breakfast is included here, too. From Central Station take tram 1 to Overtoom and then walk two blocks along Nassaukade. (Map area B6)

Get Lucky Guest House - Keizersgracht 705, 420-6466

www.getluckyamsterdam.com

While it's definitely not your average hotel (let's just say it's a little unconventional), the four cosy guest rooms in this old canal house have all been renovated and there's a computer in every room. Prices start at €40 for a single, €50 for a double without a view, €85 for a double with a canal view, and €110 for a luxurious apartment that can sleep up to five people. The location is great - close to everything. The owners are more than happy to give you tourist info, or you can hang out in the comfy media lounge (equipped with full internet and gaming facilities) and pick up some tips from other travellers. It's a good idea to book well in advance because this is a popular little place. Take tram 4 from Central Station to Keizersgracht. It's right there. (Map area E7)

The Greenhouse Effect - Warmoesstraat 55, 624-4974
www.the-greenhouse-effect.com

The 17 rooms of this smoker-friendly hotel each have a different theme (outer space, tropical island, techno, etc), making it the perfect place for the stoner traveller with a bit more money to spend on accommodation. Prices start at €60 for a single, €90 for a twin, and €120 for a triple. Every room has a colour TV and a safe, and most have a private shower and toilet. The price includes a breakfast buffet until noon, and guests are entitled to special "happy hour" prices all day on weed and booze at the hotel's coffeeshop and bar downstairs. If you're travelling with a group, look into one of the three apartments they rent. The Greenhouse Effect is located in the Red Light District, which is walking distance from Central Station. (Map area D4)

The Flying Pig - Nieuwendijk 100, 420-6822; Vossiusstraat 46-47, 400-4187
www.flyingpig.nl

Both these hostels have private rooms, too. Twins rooms with shower and toilet (but no TVs) cost €64.50 to €75; and those without facilities start at €60.50. See the Hostels section (above) for more details.

Groenendael - Nieuwendijk 15, 624-4822
www.hotelgroenendael.com

If you prefer to stay close to the centre of town, then this hotel is a good deal. Singles go for €32, doubles for €50, and triples for €75 (cheaper off season). Showers and toilets are in the hall. Breakfast is included. The rooms are tiny and pretty basic, but you're paying for the location. There's a lounge where you can hang out and meet people. The street is a little sleazy, but it's not dangerous. From Central Station, walk or run. (Map area D3)

Hotel Aspen - Raadhuisstraat 31, 626-6714
www.hotelaspen.nl

There are a bunch of hotels here in the beautiful Art Nouveau "Utrecht Building". The hotel Aspen is a small, family-run place that feels more like a guest house than a hotel. Singles here start at €33. Doubles with a sink in the room start at €43. A triple with shower and toilet goes for €75 to €80. And a quad with shower and toilet is €89. No breakfast, but a great location close to Dam Square and Anne Frank House. From Central Station take tram 6, 13 or 17 to Westermarkt and walk back half a block. If you don't have much luggage, it's only a 10 or 15 minute walk. (Map area C4)

Bed & Coffee - Rustenburgerstraat 427, 06-551-94911
www.bedcoffee.nl

Because this tiny hotel is a bit out of the centre and only has three rooms, you can stay here for the same price you'd pay for a dorm bed at a hostel. A small twin room goes for €50, and a bigger double for €60. A quad goes for €90. The shower and toilet are shared. It's very clean, and there's a cozy lounge with a TV, 24-hour internet access, and free coffee and hot chocolate. It's a smoker-friendly place, and in fact, guests get a 10% discount at the neighbourhood coffeeshop, or a free drink at the Black Sheep bar across the street. Book very early. Bed and Coffee is located in the Pijp (pipe) area. From Central Station take tram 24 or 25 to Ceintuurbaan, walk two blocks further along Ferdinand Bolstraat and turn right.

Van Ostade Bicycle Hotel - Van Ostadestraat 123, 679-3452

www.bicyclehotel.com

If you're travelling by bicycle take note. This is one of the only hotels in Amsterdam with free indoor bike parking. They also rent bikes to guests for €5 per day and provide info on tours in and out of Amsterdam. The rooms? €61 for a single. €70 to €99 for doubles. €90 to €120 for triples. €130 for a quad. Breakfast is included. The rooms aren't exciting, but they're clean and all have TVs. There's a library/lounge downstairs. It's located in the Pijp, too - a fun, lively neighbourhood. From Central Station take (or cycle behind) tram 24 or 25 and stop at Ceintuurbaan. Cross the street and go one block further.

Hotel Rembrandt - Plantage Middenlaan 17, 627-2714

www.hotelrembrandt.nl

This is a sweet little hotel in a beautiful, wealthy area of town. All the rooms have a TV and a coffee/tea maker, but if you've got the dough, splurge on the more expensive doubles (€100 per room). Each of those rooms is uniquely decorated, has a modern bathroom, and is way nicer than what you normally get for that price in Amsterdam. Other doubles cost €65 to €68 per night, with shower and toilet in the hall. Sometimes they can squeeze in an extra person for €21. Quad rooms cost €140 to €150. Breakfast is included in an incredible, antique-filled room. On weekends there's a minimum 3 night stay. Book early! The Botanical Gardens (see Museums chapter) is two minutes away, and just beyond that, the Waterlooplein market. From Central Station take tram 9 to Plantage Kerklaan and then walk back half a block. (Map area F6)

Amstel Botel - Oosterdokskade 2-4, 626-4247

www.amstelbotel.com

It's sort of unique to stay in a 4-story hotel that's that's on a boat. The rooms are small, but very clean and modern. They all have a tiny shower and toilet, a phone, and a TV with free in-house videos (including a porn channel). The reception is open 24 hours and they don't charge commission to change money. Single and double rooms cost €89 per night; triple rooms cost €98. Prices drop about €10 in the winter. Breakfast is not included. Make sure you get a room overlooking the water because the street side is ugly. Located just a couple of minutes walk east of Central Station, a walk that can be a bit creepy at night. (Map area F3)

House-Boat Hotel

www.houseboathotel.nl

Another possibility if you like the idea of sleeping on a canal, is to rent a houseboat. This website offers several boats for daily or weekly rental. If you're travelling with a small group, this sometimes works out to be comparable to the price of a hotel, but is usually much more luxurious. These boats are very popular so make sure you book well in advance. There's a €20 booking fee. Note also that for safety reasons, smoking is only allowed outside - on the balconies or in the gardens.

Arena - 's Gravesandestraat 51, 694-7444

www.hotelarena.nl

Years ago, this huge, old mansion was converted into a low-budget hostel because the City wanted hippies to stop sleeping in Vondelpark. It turned into one of the coolest hostels in town, in spite of being located a bit outside of the centre. Now the dorms are gone and they only rent rooms. Depending on the season, small doubles go for €100 to €125. Other doubles cost €125 to €175, and triples go for €140 to €165. All rooms have shower and toilet, TV, telephone, and the very important reading lights by the bed. You can rent a Playstation (€10 for 24 hours) if you need a fix of *Tony Hawk's Pro Skater*. Breakfast is included, but not a 5% tax. As always, it's a good idea to make a reservation. It's close to the Tropenmuseum and Oosterpark. From Central Station take tram 9 to Mauritskade. Night bus 76 or 77. (Map area G8)

Xaviera Hollander's B & B - Stadionweg 17, 673-3934
www.xavierahollander.com/sleeper

I know that €120 a night isn't exactly cheap, but this is the home of a real celebrity. Xaviera Hollander's house is in the wealthy area of Amsterdam south. She rents two rooms to visitors. Both have TVs and king-size beds, and of course, breakfast is included. Prices sometimes drop in off-season, or for long stays. Go to the website to see pictures of the rooms, and to read about all the creative projects Xaviera's got going. The Happy Hooker has a guest house: that had to be in *The Cool Guide*.

Black Tulip Hotel - Gelderskade 16, 427-0933
www.blacktulip.nl

I should start by saying that this hotel, situated in a 16th-century canal house near Central Station, caters exclusively to leather men. That is, gay men who are seriously into S/M, B&D and leather fetish. Each of the nine luxurious rooms is decorated differently, but all feature kinky sex equipment: metal cages, stocks, fist-fuck chairs, etc. In addition to a sling and bondage hooks, all rooms have TVs with VCRs, minibars, telephones, and private bathrooms (some with whirlpool). Prices range from €105 to €175 and include a buffet breakfast in their comfortable lounge. And, as a service to guests who prefer to travel light, they rent big, heavy, leather boots and other paraphernalia here, too. (Map area E4)

A bed at the Black Tulip

Prins Hendrik Hotel - Prins Hendrikkade 53, 623-7969

I've never been inside, but this is the hotel Chet Baker was staying in when he fell (or took a dive, or was pushed) out of his window to his death, back in '88. If you're a big fan you might want to stay here too, or - if you find that a tad morbid - visit the plaque out front commemorating one of jazz's late greats. (Map area E4)

camping

Zeeburg - Zuider IJdijk 20, 694-4430

www.campingzeeburg.nl

They have all kinds of facilities here, including a funky bar that throws regular parties in the summer. Camping costs €4 per person plus €3.50 per tent. There are also "camping huts" with beds at around €16 per person. Open all year. From Dam Square take tram 14 to the last stop at Flevopark. From there you can follow the signs which lead you over the big bridge and to the campgrounds on the right. Night bus 77 (then a 20 minute walk).

Gaasper Camping - Loosdrechtdreef 7, 696-7326

www.gaaspercamping-amsterdam.nl

€8 per adult, €3.50 per kid, €4.50 per dog (plus €8.75 for a 2-person tent, €10.75 for a 3-or-more-person tent, and €7.50 per car). Open March 15th to December 31st. Take the metro from Central Station to Gaasperplein. From there it's a five minute walk.

Vliegenbos - Meeuwenlaan 138, 636-8855

www.vliegenbos.com

Located in Amsterdam North. €7.25 per person. And you'll be charged extra if you have a vehicle. There are also 30 cabins (four beds each) that rent for €45.30 a night. They accept written reservations for the cabins from March. Open April 1st to September 30th. Buses; 32, 36. Night bus 73.

Amsterdamse Bos - Kleine Noorddijk 1, 641-6868

www.amsterdamsebos.amsterdam.nl/amsterdamsebos/camping/index.html

There's a campsite here in the beautiful woods just south of the city centre. €5 per person, €3 per tent, €3 per car. Open April 1st to October 15th. Bus 171 from Central Station. Ask the driver for the closest stop.

Getting Around

Central Amsterdam's old cobblestone streets are great for wandering through and getting lost. And fortunately, Amsterdam is full of people who speak English (to get you found). But, actually, you shouldn't have too much trouble if you take a few minutes to study a map. Detailed maps are available all over. Buy one: they're only about €2 and the street names listed on the back will make it easy to quickly find the places mentioned in this book.

If you really can't afford to buy a map, there are also a variety of free ones available around town: the Amsterdam Diamond Center (Rokin 1-5) offers maps of the city centre; both High View and the BCD (Cannabis Retailers' Association) produce advertising maps that are available in many coffeeshops; the Gay Tourist Map is free at Pink Point (see Practical Shit chapter); and at tourist locations you'll find a Visitors Guide published by the Yellow Pages that includes a pretty good map. Finally, you can always use the one found in the front pages of the telephone book - it's fairly detailed and includes a street registry.

Online, go to *www.amsterdam.nl* and click on *Stadsplattegrond*. Type in the address of your hotel or any other place in Amsterdam and it loads a printable map of the street, neighbourhood, or whole city with your destination clearly marked.

The basic layout of the city, with a series of horseshoe-shaped canals surrounding the oldest part, makes it fairly easy to find your way on foot. This is certainly the best way to see Amsterdam and fully appreciate its incredible beauty.

bicycles

Buttman at a bike demo.

Don't be scared to rent a bike and go for an authentic Amsterdam experience. Unlike most North American and many European cities, bikes are respected in Amsterdam. There are still too many dirty, ugly, polluting cars in the city centre, but there are also thousands of beautiful, clean, fast, efficient bicycles. There are bike lanes all over the city and it's a fun, relatively safe way to explore. Listed below are several places to rent bikes. If you're here for awhile you may want to consider buying a used bike and selling it to someone when you leave. Make sure you lock your bike everywhere, even if you're only leaving it for an instant (see note on bike theft). One of the cheapest places to buy a lock is the Waterlooplein flea market (see Markets, Shopping chapter).

Over the past couple of years, in an effort to "clean up the city" (whatever that means) there've been several crackdowns on illegal bike parking (I'm not joking). So if you see a sign that says *"geen fietsen plaatsen"* or *"fietsen worden verdwijderd"*; or notice that an area is conspicuously free of any other parked bikes, you're probably better off locking up somewhere else.

I've never been on an organized bike tour in Amsterdam, but if you're more comfortable riding with a group, Mike's Bike Tours (622-7970; *www.mikesbiketours.com*) does a trip that takes you through the inner-city and out to the countryside. From the beginning of April until the end of October the tours leave daily from entrance "B" of the Rijksmuseum. The cost is €22.

A fun day to get on a bike is the annual Autovrije Zondag (Auto-free Sunday; *www.autovrijezondag.nl*). It takes place in mid to late September, and even though the cab drivers are still allowed to drive like idiots through the city, a good portion of the centre is closed to motorized traffic.

Macbike - Central Station, 625-3845; Mr. Visserplein 2, 620-0985; Marnixstraat 220, 626 6964; Weteringschans 2 (by Leidseplein), 528-7688

www.macbike.nl

Macbike has good quality bikes and a good reputation, but sometimes there are long lines to pick-up and return rentals. They sell maps and information on cycling routes in and outside the city (€1). Standard bikes cost €6.50 per business day (not 24 hours). Bikes with hand-brakes and gears cost €9.75 per business day. The more days you rent the cheaper it gets. A €50 deposit or a credit card slip, plus a passport, is required. Theft insurance (optional) costs an extra 50%. Open: daily 9-18. (Map areas B5, E6, C7, B7)

Bike City - Bloemgracht 70, 626-3721

www.bikecity.nl

This is a genuinely friendly shop located on a beautiful canal near the Anne Frank House. Standard bikes cost €6.75 per business day (not 24 hours), €29.50 for 5 days, and €4.50 for each additional day. They also rent 3-speed bikes with hand brakes (€8.50 per day) and 5-speed mountain bikes (€10.50 per day). If you request it, you'll be provided with a puncture repair kit - a bonus if you're heading for the countryside. You'll be asked for a passport and a cash deposit of €25 (or a credit card slip). Open: daily 9-18. Closed during the x-mas and new years period. (Map area B4)

Rent-A-Bike-Damstraat - Damstraat 20, 625-5029

www.bikes.nl

You'll find Rent-A-Bike in an alley off Damstraat just east of Dam Square. They're also very friendly. Keep your eyes peeled for their small coupons that get you a 10% discount. The only drawback to renting here is the big sign on the front of their bikes that screams "tourist". You can rent by the hour (€3.50 for the first hour, then cheaper for each additional hour), or by the day (€7 from 9 to 18:00 or €9.50 for 24 hours). Their special weekly rate is €31. They require a €25 deposit (cash or credit card) and a passport. Seats and helmets for kids are also available. Open: daily 9-18. (Map area D5)

Frédéric Rent a Bike - Brouwersgracht 78, 624-5509

www.frederic.nl

It's just a 10-minute walk from Central Station to this small shop. They charge €10 a day (24 hours) and the price includes insurance and a child-seat, if you need it. They don't ask for a deposit, just a credit card or passport. And there's no advertising on their bikes, which is a nice touch. They also organize room rentals in several houses and boats in the neighbourhood and the prices are pretty good. Open: daily 9-18. (Map area D3)

Binnenpret - 1e Schinkelstraat 14, tel: 0651-720911

One place to buy a cheap bike is at the shop in a shed in the courtyard of this old squat at the far end of Vondelpark (see OCCII, Live Venues, Music chapter). The guy who runs it sells very basic, refurbished bikes for about €50. He may have one on hand, but often you have to place an order and then pick it up later. They're not great bikes, but they should hold up for the duration of your stay. Usually open: mon-fri 12-19.

Via Via - 626-6166

www.viavia.nl

Via Via is a classified ads paper that's published every Tuesday and Thursday. It features thousands of articles for sale and is available all over town. Look under *Fietsen* or *Tweewielers*. There are always lots of cheap bikes listed, though you'll have to find a Dutch speaker to help you read the ads. The paper costs €2.40, but you can peruse it at the library for free (see Hanging Out chapter).

BMX

Though there's always some rivalry with the skaterboarders, all the spots mentioned for skateboarding in the Hanging Out chapter get used by BMX bikers too. But to get the most up-to-date info on what's really happening on the scene, check out Soul Cycle (Nieuwe Herengracht 33; 771-5484; *www.soulcycle.nl*). They're in the middle of it all. (Map area E6)

Bike Wars - Vondel Park; every couple of months

Bike demolition derby. Every couple of months a bunch of people meet at night at the open air theatre in Vondelpark (see Parks, Hanging Out chapter), and with some heavy tunes playing in the background they ride around and smash the crap out of each others bikes until only one is still ride-able. Cool.

inline skates

Rodolfo's - Sarphatistraat 59, 622-5488

www.rodolfos.nl

Inline skates for rent! Skating is not bad on the bike lanes and the people who work here at Europe's oldest skateshop know all the hot spots around town. The rental is from 12 noon 'til 11:00 the next day, and the price is €7.50. A €100 deposit and ID, or a credit card, is required. They also sell snowboards, skateboards, and skate fashions. Open: mon 13-18; tues-fri 10-18 (thurs 'til 21); sat 10-17. (Map area E8)

Rent A Skate - Vondelpark, 664-5091

www.vondeltuin.nl

Vondelpark (see Hanging Out chapter) is the best place to skate, especially if you're inexperienced and want to avoid traffic. Skates are rented by the café at the Amstelveenseweg end of Vondelpark. You'll need €5/hour plus a passport and a €20 deposit. They're open daily (when the streets are dry) from March to October, 11 to sunset; and on weekends from mid-March to May.

Friday Night Skate - Vondelpark

www.fridaynightskate.nl

As long as the roads are dry, skaters meet every Friday evening at 20:00 just to the right of the Film Museum in Vondelpark and head out for a 15 kilometre tour through the city. Everyone is welcome, but you should be an experienced skater. (Map area B8)

public transport

Most people visiting Amsterdam stay mainly in the centre and don't have to rely too much on public transit. But if you need it, you'll find there's a good network of trams, buses and metro lines. The transit system operates largely on the honour system, so you can try to ride for free if you want, but if you get caught the "I'm a tourist; I didn't understand" routine usually won't work. The fine is about €30 plus the fare. And by law you have to show them some ID.

Amsterdam is divided into zones, and the more zones you travel in the more expensive your ticket will be. If you'll be using public transit for more than one round trip your best bet is to buy a 15-strip *"strippenkaart"* for €6.20. Most of central Amsterdam is one zone. For each ride in the centre you must stamp two strips on your card. You can do it yourself in one of the yellow boxes you'll find in most trams and metro stations, or you can ask the driver or tram conductor to do it for you. Your ticket is then valid for an hour within that zone (the last in the series of numbers stamped on your ticket is the time you embarked). You have to stamp an extra strip for each additional zone you want to travel in or through - one zone costs two strips, two zones cost three strips, etc. Buy these *strippenkaarten* at Central Station, post offices, tobacco shops and supermarkets. Single tickets can be purchased on trams and buses, but they're much more expensive (€1.60). You can also purchase day tickets that are good on all buses, trams, and the metro (subway) from 1- 9 days (1 day - €5.20; 2 days - €8.30; 3 days - €10.70). After midnight, night buses take over, but only on some routes, and the prices go up. To disembark your train, tram or bus, push the button by the door.

In addition to the regular buses and trams, Amsterdam now has a wonderful mini-bus service called the *Opstapper* that runs every 10 minutes from Central Station, along the Brouwersgracht, Prinsengracht, Amstel, and ends at the Stopera (see Free Concerts, Hanging Out chapter), which is where the Waterlooplein flea market is. There are no stops: you can flag it down and get on or off anywhere along the route. It's a one-zone fare and you can use your strippenkaart. (Hours of service: mon-sat 7:30-18:30.)

For more information about public transit (or help finding your way somewhere), visit the GVB ticket office and pick up a free route map. Walk across the little square in front of Central Station and you'll see it on your left - in the same building as the Tourist Office. (It's open: mon-fri 7-21; sat/sun 8-21.) You can also call 0900-9292 for directions, but it costs €.50 per minute and I've found that they often give bad advice. Perhaps it's a feeble attempt to get the public to support the privatization of public transit.

And now that I'm bitching, you might be interested to know that the big construction messes that you'll encounter all over the city for the next decade or so is work on a new "North/South" subway line. It's one of those extremely unpopular, ill-conceived mega-projects that steadily leeches millions from education and other social services. You know, the kind of project that stays alive in spite of safety concerns, serious doubts about its necessity, and ongoing allegations of massive fraud. See, there are some similarities between Amsterdam and the city you come from.

cars

Parking

There are already too many fucking cars in Amsterdam, but if you *have* to bring one into the city the best thing to do is put it in a garage and leave it there. It's expensive, but nowhere near as much as if you get caught parking illegally. The most reasonably priced is the Arena/Transferium (tel: 400-1721), a huge garage under a stadium south of the city centre (from the A10 take exit A9/A2 and turn off at Ouderkerk aan de Amstel). Parking there costs €1.50 an hour; €14.50 a day. Ask at the counter and they'll give you two free metro (subway) tickets to the centre and back. Innercity parking is much more expensive. At the Museumplein lot (Entrance off Van Baerlestraat, 427-8398), the price is €2.50 an hour in the day, and €1.50 an hour at night, to a maximum of €27.50 a day. They're open to park sun-wed from 7 to 1:00, and thurs-sat from 7 to 2:30, but you can exit anytime. (Map area B8). ANVB Parking (Prins Hendrikkade 20a, 638-5330) costs even more - €2.50/hour; €30/day - but it's open 24 hours. (Map area D3). For a list of all the parking garages in Amsterdam, along with maps and prices, check online at: *www.naaramsterdam.nl/engels*

From 9 until midnight (noon to midnight on Sundays), parking on the street in the centre costs an average of €3 an hour, depending on the neighbourhood you're in and the time of day. You pay at little blue boxes that are on every block, and the instructions are in English. The further out you go, the cheaper the price. There are still a few areas outside of the centre with free street parking (Buikslotermeerplein, Diemen Zuid, Gaasperplas, Watergraafsmeer), but by the time you read this, that may be history.

Warning: wheel clamping of illegally parked cars is very common in Amsterdam. If you have a credit card you can call 553-0700 and someone will come and unclamp your car. If you only have cash you'll have to go to an inconveniently located office to pay your ticket (about €68) and then wait for someone to come around and unclamp your car. If you leave it for more than 24 hours, your car will be towed. Then you can expect to pay over €200 to get it back!

Car Rental

If you want to rent a car, look in the yellow pages under *Autoverhuur*. One of the best deals going is easyCar (Wibautstraat 224; Schiphol airport; *www.easycar.com*). Booking must be done online and prices can be less than €10 a day. But watch out for extra charges like €3 for paying with a credit card, and a whopping €16 if you bring the car back dirty. Kuperus, in the east end (Van der Madeweg 1, 668-3311) have small cars starting at €20 per day, but the guys who work there are exceedingly unpleasant. It might be worth it to pay a bit more somewhere else. I once got a good deal from Sixt (Amsteldijk 52; 470-8883). Avoid Adams Rent a Car Service. Note that if you can provide an Amsterdam address for the rental agreement, you might get a better deal from the major rental companies as some have special rates for residents.

24 Hour Gas Stations

There are gas stations open 24 hours at Sarphatistraat 225 and Marnixstraat 250. Please remember when you're buying gas, that Shell Oil helped prop up the apartheid regime in South Africa. They also supported the corrupt military dictatorship in Nigeria that murdered Ken Saro-Wiwa and so many other Ogoni people. Shell isn't the only sleazy oil company around, but they are the target of a world-wide boycott. Hit the greedy bastards where it hurts them the most: in their pockets.

Taxis

They're expensive, and they treat cyclists like shit, but if you really need one call 677-7777 and enjoy the service: *these* taxis are very comfortable. You can sometimes flag one down on the street, but usually you have to go to a taxi stand. You'll find them at: Central Station, Dam Square, Leidseplein, Rembrandtplein, Nieuwmarkt, Haarlemmerpoort, the Tropenmuseum, etc.

If you're alone and without much luggage, try calling Small Cab (0900-762-5522; *www.small-cab.com*). You have to pay €.22 a minute to call, but they use cool little Smart cars that are smoke-free, and they're much cheaper than regular taxis.

boats

Tours

Boat tours leave from several docks in front of Central Station and along the Damrak and Rokin. It's very touristy, but I think it's fun to see the city from the canal perspective, and some of the taped info is interesting. The tours usually give you a quick look at the harbour and then cruise along the canals while a recording in four languages describes the sights. The routes vary slightly, last one hour, depart every twenty minutes or so, and cost about €8. One company, Lovers, has a printable coupon on their website (*www.lovers.nl*) that gets you a €2 discount. The canals are particularly beautiful at night. The last tours depart at 22:00 and are often sold out in advance during high season.

Ferries

Behind Central Station, you'll find free ferries that make the brief journey to North Amsterdam every few minutes. You can take your bike on with you and it's a good starting point if you want to ride out into the countryside. Most of the bike rental places will give you free info about scenic routes.

Canal Bikes - 626-5574

www.canalbike.nl

Canal bikes, 2-4 person pedal bikes, are all over the old city canals in summer and look like a lot of fun. They can be rented at several locations, including in front of the Rijksmuseum, near Leidseplein, and Anne Frank House. One or two people pay €7/hour each; 3 or more people pay €6/hour each. Deposit: €50. Open: in summer 10-18 ('til 21:30 if the weather is really nice); and in winter, at the dock opposite the Rijksmuseum, 10-17:30.

A NOTE ON BIKE THIEF MOTHERFUCKERS

Last year in Amsterdam over 100,000 bikes were stolen. Hot bikes are sold by sorry-looking junkies who cruise around mumbling "*fiets te koop*", but more bikes are actually stolen by organised gangs. Junkies sell hot bikes very cheaply, but if you're tempted to buy one while you're here, think again. When you buy a stolen bike you're hurting the person who owned it, as well as keeping the asshole who nicked it in business. You can also get busted: the cops are cracking down on bike theft by arresting people when they buy a stolen bicycle.

Getting Out
of Amsterdam

train

Travelling by train is certainly the most pleasant and comfortable way to get around Europe, but it can also be very expensive. On some routes you have to reserve a seat (and pay a reservation fee) even if the train isn't full, which seems kind of ludicrous; but in the summertime it's a good idea to book a seat even if it isn't mandatory. The booking office for international train journeys is upstairs on platform 2a in Central Station. Grab a number and be prepared to wait. Tickets for destinations within Holland can be purchased on the ground floor, just to the left as you enter the main hall of the station, or from the big yellow machines (which have instructions in English). Neither the ticket office nor the machines take credit cards. For international train info and reservations by phone, call 0900-9296 (€.25/min); for trains within the Netherlands, dial 0900-9292 (€.50/min). Online, go to: *www.ns.nl*. The website also provides information about special deals on rail travel in Holland.

Thalys - 0900-9296 (€.25/min)

www.thalys.com

Here's a tip. If you're planning to go from Amsterdam to Paris, you can ride this high-speed train from Central Station to Gare du Nord for less than €80 return. It's a little more expensive than the bus, but takes only about half the time (4 hours), and it's much more comfortable. There are only a few seats offered at this price on each train, however, so book early.

bus

Eurolines - Rokin 10; Amstel Station, 560-8788

www.eurolines.nl

Eurolines has service to almost 500 destinations. I've had both good and bad experiences with this company, but they are much cheaper than the train, especially off-season. Check it out early because not all routes are served daily and they often sell out in advance. Keep in mind that border checks, especially going into France, tend to be a lot more severe on buses than on other modes of transport. You need to provide your passport number to buy a ticket. Rokin office open: mon-fri 9:30-17:30 (thurs 'til 20); sat 11-17. Amstel Station office open: mon-fri 7-22:30. (Map area D5)

hitching

There is a lot of competition hitching out of Amsterdam in the summer, but people do give lifts. Hitching isn't allowed on the national highways. Stay on the on-ramps or in gas stations. You'll avoid hassles from the cops and, anyway, it's easier for drivers to pick you up. If you're heading to Utrecht, take tram 25 to the end of the line and join the crowd on the Utrechtseweg. How about southern or central Germany? Hop the metro to Amstel station and try your luck on the Gooiseweg. For Rotterdam and The Hague go by tram 4 to the RAI convention centre and walk down Europaboulevard until you see the entrance to the A2 highway. But before you hit the road, check *www.hitchhikers.org* and see if you can arrange a ride without breathing exhaust. Good luck.

air travel

Budget Travel Agencies

There are several budget travel agencies south of Dam Square (going *away* from Central Station). Budget Air is at Rokin 34 (627-1251). Air-Fair (Rokin 52, 620-5121, *www.airfare.nl*) is just a bit further up and sometimes has good prices on flights, and also on package deals. For last-minute specials (mostly to southern Europe and North Africa) pop into L'tur at Heiligeweg 7 (320-5783; *www.ltur-ams.com*), or visit their counter at Schiphol Airport. Martinair also has a counter at Schiphol Airport (601-1767; *www.martinair.com*) where tickets for last-minute flights can be purchased. I had a good experience recently at D-reizen (Linnaeusstraat 112; 200-1012), which is part of a big chain. They've got last-minute deals on various airlines for two people travelling together. World Ticket Center (Nieuwezijds Voorburgwal 159, 626-1011) sometimes has special offers and the consultants there are very nice. Note that all travel agencies in Amsterdam tack on a ridiculous, rip-off, "service charge" of about €15 per person! For a complete listing of travel agencies look in the phone book (the white pages) under *Reisbureau*. Shop around.

easyJet

www.easyjet.com

Like all airlines, they suck. But at least easyJet isn't expensive. Book online with a credit card and you can get some dirt cheap fares. You can fly one way from Amsterdam, including all taxes, to London for €22, Nice for €30, and Barcelona for €40! They fly to several other destinations as well. There's no ticket: just print your confirmation and bring it to the airport.

Basiq Air

www.basiqair.com

Basiq Air flies from Amsterdam to southern France and Spain. You have to pay for all food and drinks, and they don't have any extras like newspapers or pillows, but they're cheap.

Virgin Express

www.virgin-express.com

Cheap flights from Amsterdam to Southern Europe, and soon, hopefully, to North America as well.

Call and Go - tel: 023-567-4567

This phone line (run by the Dutch airline, KLM) is updated daily with good deals on next-day departures to all sorts of destinations. The recorded message is available from 13 to 23:00 and it's in Dutch and English. If you stay on the line after the message ends, you'll be connected with KLM reservations. Unfortunately, there are only return tickets on offer and the maximum stay is 4 weeks. And KLM also charges you €25 to make a reservation on the phone. What a scam! A better bet is to book through their website (*www.klm.nl*), where, along with the Call and Go deals, they now list youth and student fares as well.

Train to the Airport

Easy as pie! Hop on the train at Central Station (€3.10) and you're at Schiphol Airport (*www.schiphol.nl*) in about 20 minutes. Trains depart regularly starting at about 4:45 in the morning until just after midnight. After that there's just one train per hour. Keep a close eye on your luggage! (Did you know that Schiphol Airport is five metres below sea level?).

Bus to the Airport

The Interliner Bus rides between Leidseplein and the airport, and costs €2.50 one-way, and €4.20 return. It leaves every 30 minutes, 24 hours a day. Call 0900-9292 (€.50/min) for exact departure times. It's a bit cheaper than the train, but then you have to spend a euro on the phone getting the information!

maps & travel books

à la Carte - Utrechtsestraat 110-112, 625-0679

Open: mon 13-18; tues-fri 10-18 (in summer, thurs 'til 21); sat 10-17. (Map area E7)

Pied à Terre - Singel 393, 627-4455　　　　　　　　　　**www.piedaterre.nl**

Open: mon-fri 11-18 (thurs 'til 21, apr 1- sept 1); sat 10-17. (Map area C5)

Boekhandel Jacob van Wijngaarden - Overtoom 97, 612-1901　　　**www.jvw.nl**

Open: mon 13-18; tues-fri 10-18 (thurs 'til 21); sat 10-17. (Map area A7)

Evenaar - Singel 348, 624-6289　　　　　　　　**http://travel.to/evenaar**

(See Books & Magazines, Shopping chapter) Open: mon-fri 12-18; sat 11-17. (Map area C5)

getting to the beach

Trains to Zandvoort (on the coast), leave from Central Station approximately every half hour. In the summer there are direct trains and on sunny days they're very crowded. Off-season you have to change trains in Haarlem. The trip takes about 30 minutes and costs €4.10 one-way and €7.20 return. You can bring your bike for an extra charge (about €6 return). Zandvoort can get very crowded, the water isn't exactly clean, and it's often very windy. But the beach is big, wide and white, and a day trip there can be a lot of fun. For the past few years, the hot party place to hang has been at Bloemendaal aan Zee, a 45 minute walk north along the beach from Zandvoort. Several pavillions there host regular parties. It's a bit of a meat market, but it can also be a relaxing place to kick back, listen to the music, and watch the sunset. Sometimes there's a beach-shuttle that'll take you there for about €2, but usually you have to hoof it along the beach. Remember to check the departure time of the last train back to Amsterdam!

Practical Shit

tourist info

The Amsterdam Tourist Office (a.k.a. the VVV) is the city's official tourist agency. However, it's also a privately-run business, so even though the people working here are almost always patient and friendly, and can be very helpful, you can see that the word from on high is "sell, sell, sell". There's a branch inside Central Station, upstairs on platform 2 (open: mon-sat 8-20; sun 9-17), and another just to the left as you cross the square in front of the station (open: daily 9-17). There's also a branch at Leidseplein (open: mon-sat 9-19; sun 9-17). Be prepared for a long wait if you're here during high season. They have an info number, but it's very expensive (0900-400-4040; mon-fri 9-17; €.55 per minute). (Map area E3)

money

While there may be valid arguments for a single European currency, you know that the old white guys in suits that made this a done deal didn't do it for the benefit of you and me. The euro (€) is now the official currency in the Netherlands. You don't have to change money now when you travel between member countries, but you pay higher prices for everything.

I hate fucking banks! They're all thieves and scum. However, changing money at bank alternatives in the tourist areas (like Leidseplein) is mostly a big rip-off, too: high commission charges and low rates. Beware of places that advertise "no commission" in big letters followed by fine print that says "if you're purchasing" (this means if you're giving them euros to buy US $, for example). It's a scam, and once they have your money inside their bullet-proof glass booth you won't get it back. It's hard to recommend a place because they're changing all the time, but here are a few stable money-changers.

Lorentz Change - Damrak 31, 420-2343; Nieuwendijk 80, 528-9944

These guys offer the best rates on cash, and no commission on non-euro currencies. Open: daily, 24 hours. (Map area D4)

Pott-Change - Damrak 95, 626-3658; Rembrandtplein 10, 626-8768

There's no commission charged here, either, if you're changing non-euro currencies. And their fee for cashing non-euro travellers cheques is relatively low. Open: mon-sat 8-20; sun 9-20. (Map area D4)

American Express - Damrak 66, 504-8777

If you're wanting them cashed out in euros, Amex doesn't charge a fee to process their own travellers' cheques. Open: mon-fri 9-17; sat 9-12. (Map area D4)

Thomas Cook - Damrak 1, 620-3236

Again, if you're wanting euros, Thomas Cook will process their own cheques free of charge. Watch out, though: they charge a high fee to change cash. Open: mon-sat 8-20; sun 9-20. (Map area E3)

GWK Bank - Central Station, 627-2731

This member of the bank mafia charges 2.25% commission on the total cash amount changed, plus an extra €2.25. And the fee for changing travellers' cheques is even more. It's a rip-off - but they're open late if you're stuck. Open: daily 7-22:45 (Map area E3)

phone

To use a phone booth you'll need a phone card. They can be purchased in denominations of €5 and €10 at the Tourist Office, post offices, tobacco shops, and supermarkets. Phone booths have instructions in English. Pay phones that take coins are almost extinct, with old-school bars and cafés just about their only remaining habitat.

For long distance calls dial 00, then your country code and the number. Holland's country code is 31. Amsterdam's city code is 20 from abroad and 020 if you're dialling from elsewhere in The Netherlands. Long-distance phone cards are available in most of the "call centres" on tourist strips like the Damrak, and at tobacco shops. They come in different denominations and they can be a very good deal. Easy-to-use instructions, in English, are printed on the back of the cards.

If you have a mobile phone and the battery is low, some of the phone shops on the Rokin (like Dutchtone, Rokin 64a) will let you plug in and charge it for free.

post

The Dutch postal service has been privatized, which has led to higher prices and the closure of hundreds of offices all over Holland. There are now only a couple of outlets left in Amsterdam's city centre and they're always very crowded. The **main post office** is located at Singel 250 (556-3311), at the corner of Raadhuisstraat, just west of Dam Square. If you're just buying some stamps or something else quick, you can line up at the express counter - number 1. Otherwise, take a number and be prepared to wait a while. Postcards take €.39 stamps. Letters up to 20 grams cost €.59 for Europe and €.75 overseas. There's also a stationary store here, and a bank that changes money (though they're very slow and charge commission). The main post office is open: mon-fri 9-18 (thurs 'til 20); sat 10-13:30. (Map area C4)

The entrance to the **Poste Restante** is down some stairs to the left of the entrance to the main post office. If you're having mail sent to you the address is: Poste Restante, Hoofdpostkantoor PTT, Singel 250, 1012 SJ, Amsterdam, The Netherlands. Don't forget to bring your passport when you go to pick up your letters. Open: mon-fri 9-18:30; sat 9-12.

There are also post offices at Waterlooplein 2 (inside city hall), and Haarlemmerdijk 97, but note that their opening hours are often shorter than those of the main office listed above. Some supermarkets also sell stamps from vending machines near their entrances. Before or after regular hours, head to the sorting centre just east of Central Station (Oosterdokskade 3). You can buy stamps there from 7:30 to 20:00 on weekdays, and on Saturday from 7:30 'til 12:00. For more postal info, call the **free customer service line**: 058-233-3333 (choose "9" to speak to a human).

If you're posting letters from a **mailbox**, the right-hand slot is for Amsterdam, and the left side is for the rest of the world.

If you want to send or receive e-mail stop by one of the internet cafés or the main library (see Hanging Out chapter).

left luggage

The lockers at Central Station cost €2.50 (small) and €4.50 (large) for 24 hours. The maximum rental period is 72 hours at a time. The locker area is closed at night from 1 to 5:00. If your stuff is too big for the lockers, there's a left-luggage counter that charges €5.70 per piece for 24 hours. It's a rip-off, but what can you do? They're open daily from 7 'til 23:00 and the maximum storage time permitted is 10 days.

Warning: like all big train stations the world over, Central Station has its share of bag-snatchers hanging about. Never take your eyes off your luggage - even for a second.

voltage

The electric current in Holland operates on 220 volts. If you're from Canada or the U.S., you'll have to get a converter and/or a transformer if you want to plug in anything that you've brought with you. Note that it's probably cheaper to buy them in North America than in Holland.

weather

Expect lousy weather. Then if it's warm and dry, you'll feel really lucky (which you will be). Bring layers of clothing and something waterproof. Umbrellas don't always do the trick, as this is a very windy country, especially in the fall. The North Sea wind also means that the weather can change very quickly and several times a day. Winters are cold, but it rarely goes much below freezing. July and August are your best bet for nice weather (of course). Having said all that, Amsterdam is a fun city to visit any time of year.

tipping

Tipping isn't really part of Dutch culture, and service is supposed to be included in the price at restaurants and cafes. But if you have a nice waiter you can round up the bill to the next €.50 or euro: 5% is sufficient; 10% is generous. At bars you can round up a bit, but it's not necessary to tip on every order. And if you don't have much dough it's perfectly acceptable not to tip at all.

toilets

You often have to pay to use public toilets in Europe. There's usually an attendant on duty who collects the €.25 or €.50 required, and who's supposed to be keeping things clean. It's not a lot of money, but it sure does piss me off (excuse the pun). Expensive hotels are good places to find free, clean toilets. Just walk in looking confident and head straight in past the reception desk. There's always a washroom nearby. (I like The Grand - Oudezijds Voorburgwal 197). Also, if you can handle it, you can take a whizz for free in any police station. And guys should think twice before peeing in the canals or alleys: not only are you acting like a pig, but you're risking an €86 fine if a cop spots you.

recycling

Bring your old batteries to any supermarket. Toss them into the box with a picture of a battery on it that you'll see near the entrance. It only takes a second. Glass and paper recycling bins (marked *glasbak* and *papierbak*) are found on street corners every few blocks or so.

laundry

The Wash Company - Haarlemmerdijk 132

Wash €5; dry (only in combo with wash) €.20 for 6 minutes. Wash/dry/fold service takes 4 hours and costs €7 for 6kg. Open: daily (except thurs) 9:30-18:30; sun 11:30-18:30. (Map area C2)

Wasserette - Oude Doelenstraat 12

Do-it-yourself. Five kilos for €5. Seven kilos for €7. Includes soap, wash and dry. Open: mon-fri 8:30-19 (last wash in at 17:45); sat 10-17 (last wash in at 15:45). (Map area D5)

Wash-o-matic - Pieter Langendijk 12

Out near Vondelpark you can do a load of up to 8kg for €5. Dryers cost €.20 for 6 minutes. Open: daily 8-20 (last wash in at 19:00).

pickpockets

Amsterdam is a very safe city and the only crime you're likely to witness or experience is pick-pocketing. It's not a violent crime, but what a drag when it happens! Watch out for these assholes: they're very good at what they do. Keep your valuables safely stashed and watch your bags at all times. The worst areas are around Central Station, Dam Square, Leidseplein, and the Red Light District - in other words, tourist areas where you'll probably end up at least a couple of times during your stay. They also work on public transit and the trains (especially to and from Schiphol airport). Try not to act like a total space cadet (in spite of how you might feel) and you probably won't have any problems. (If you do, see the Phone Numbers chapter for the services you'll need.)

drug testing

Hard drugs are illegal in Holland. Buying them from strangers can be dangerous. And anything you buy on the street is guaranteed to be crap. But if you've scored some ecstasy elsewhere and want to be sure that it's okay, call the Stichting Adviesburo Drugs (623-7943). *They do not sell drugs.* It's a non-profit foundation that, among other things, will test your ecstasy to see what it really is. A test costs only a few euros. They take a sliver as a sample (you won't lose your hit), and within a couple of minutes they can tell you what you've bought. This is a fantastic service (anonymous too, by the way). By testing ecstasy they know what's on the market, and if something bad is going around they can help track it down and get it out of circulation. Open: tues-fri 14-17.

gay & lesbian info

The *Cool Guide* has never included a chapter geared specifically towards lesbian and gay visitors to Amsterdam. Instead, I've made a point of highlighting a couple of spots that cater to a mainly gay crowd in each section of the book (and any place that wasn't gay-friendly, wouldn't be listed). However, to find out more about what's happening on the gay scene around town, your first stop should be the fabulous Pink Point kiosk at Westermarkt (just in front of the Homomonument). They provide all sorts of free info including the *Gay News*, and the monthly fanzine *Shark*, which features an index of alternative queer venues and events. Pink Point also sells guidebooks and all kinds of unique queer souvenirs. Open: daily 12-18; April to September. (Map area C4)

A NOTE ABOUT SQUATTING IN AMSTERDAM

If a building in Amsterdam remains empty for more than a year without the owner putting it to some use, it can be squatted. This law is meant to protect the city from speculators who sit on their property while prices rise due to the severe housing shortage.

That doesn't mean that squatters have an easy time taking over a building. The legal definition of occupancy is a slippery one, and it's difficult to have a building defined as vacant. In addition, a great deal of work is usually needed to make a squat habitable and often legal battles ensue.

I have a lot of respect for those who have chosen to live as squatters as an expression of their political beliefs. They are simultaneously working to preserve and create housing in this overcrowded city. Several of these organised squats have opened restaurants and clubs that are among the best in Amsterdam. Many of them live under imminent threat of being forced out by banks and developers. Going to these squats is a way of showing your support for a creative, co-operative way of living as well as your opposition to conservative pigs who care more about money than people.

For more information about squatting look online at *http://squat.net*. And for up-to-date info about events in squats, check out the excellent and user-friendly database at *http://radar.squat.net*

food
Food

Eating out in Amsterdam is, on the whole, expensive - particularly since the introduction of the euro. But if you pay attention to this chapter I promise you a full belly at the best price.

If you're on the tightest budget, head to the markets for the cheapest fruit, veggies, and cheese. I've listed several in the shopping chapter. For dry goods, go to the large supermarkets and remember to bring your own bags.

If you've got access to a kitchen you might want to visit a *tropische winkel* (tropical shop) for inspiration. They're found throughout the city, especially near the markets, and they specialize in foods from tropical countries: everything from mangoes to hot sauce to cassava chips.

supermarkets

Supermarkets in Amsterdam are now open much longer hours than they used to be (in general: mon-sat 8-20; thurs 'til 21). At some you can even shop 'til 22:00; and more and more are staying open on Sundays, too. At some stores you have to weigh produce yourself. Push the button marked "*bon*" and a sticker with the price pops out of the scale. If there's no "*bon*" button on the scale, it means that they'll weigh it at the check-out. At Albert Heijn supermarkets pick up a free, plastic "bonus card". You'll need it to buy anything on sale: without it you'll be charged the full price. Just ask for one at the front counter (where they sell film) and they'll give you a card right away. Anyone can use it - just give it to the cashier every time you check out.

Aldi - Nieuwe Weteringstraat 26

This is one of the cheapest, but they don't have as good a selection as the bigger chains and they don't carry any organic products. Also, it's a bit hard to find and a bit grungy. (Map area C8)

Lidl - Hemonylaan 23

These small supermarkets are also cheap, but better than Aldi. This one is about a block away from the Albert Cuyp market.

Dirk van den Broek - Heinekenplein

Another cheapie, but they're starting to stock organic products. Big. American-style. Behind the Heineken Brewery. (Map area D8)

Albert Heijn

Every time I blink there's a new one. My friend calls them Adolf Heijns, because of the way they've conquered Holland and now occupy every neighbourhood. However, they carry lots of organic products (look for labels marked "*bio*"), and all the branches listed below stay open until 22:00 ('til 19 on sun). They're slick and well-stocked, but also expensive. Remember to get a "bonus card" before you shop (see intro text above). If you've got access to an oven, try their frozen, organic pizza for only €2.25.

Nieuwezijds Voorburgwal - Behind Dam Square. (Map area D5)

Koningsplein - (Map area C6)

Haarlemmerdijk 1 - 10 minute walk from Central Station. Only open 'til 21. (Map area C3)

Jodenbreestraat 20 - By the Waterlooplein flea market. (Map area E5)

Central Station - In the west tunnel by Shakies (see Street Food, below). More expensive than their bigger stores, but convenient if you're catching a train. (Open 'til 22 on sun, too).

health food stores

De Natuurwinkel - Weteringschans 133, 638-4083 (also: Haarlemmerdijk 174; 1e Constantijn Huygensstraat 49; 1e van Swindenstraat 30)

> Health food, supermarket style. A huge selection including organic produce, cheese, and baked goods. Big, busy bulletin board. If you buy fruit or vegetables here, look for the number next to each item. Then punch in the number when you weigh it. Next push the button marked "*bon*" and a sticker will come out with the price. It's less complicated than it sounds and you won't be embarrassed at the check-out when they send you back to do it. Weteringschans branch (near the Rijksmuseum) open: mon-fri 7-20 (thurs 'til 21); sat 7-20; sun 11-18. (Map area D8)

De Bast - Huidenstraat 19, 624-8087

> Located on a street full of cute shops and restaurants, De Bast carries a selection of whole grain breads as well as all the other healthy stuff. Open: mon 11:30-18:30; tues-fri 9:30-18:30; sat 9-17. (Map area C6)

Weegschaal - Jodenbreestraat 20, 624-1765

> You'll find all kinds of delicious, healthy foods in this small neighbourhood store: from macrobiotic products, to organic fruit and veggies, to taco chips. It's just around the corner from the Waterlooplein market (see Shopping chapter). Open: mon-fri 9-18; sat 9-17. (Map area E6)

De Belly - Nieuwe Leliestraat 174, 330-9483

> A sweet, well-laid-out shop that's been in business for almost 30 years. They guarantee that all their organic products are GM free! It's just a few doors down from the veggie restaurant Vliegende Schotel (see Restaurants, below). Open: mon-fri 8:30-18:30; sat 8:30-17:30. (Map area B4)

't Zonnemeer - Nieuwe Kerkstraat 8, 625-1223

This is a small, but pleasant shop with all kinds of healthy foods. They're just a stone's throw away from the beautiful "Skinny Bridge". Open: mon-fri 8:30-18; sat 8:30-17. (Map area E7)

De Aanzet - Frans Hals Straat 27, 673-3415

This pretty, cooperatively-run store is not far from the Albert Cuyp market (see Markets, Shopping chapter). They stock some bulk products, organic fruits and veggies, and yummy baked goods. Open: mon-fri 9-18; sat 9-17.

Natura Oase - Jan Pieter Heijestraat 105, 618-2887

If you're in Vondelpark and you need some picnic fixin's, stop by this neighbourhood health food store. And bring an empty bottle because they also have organic wine on tap! Open: mon-fri 8-18; sat 8-17.

street foods

Falafel stands are scattered all about the city. Maoz Falafel (see Restaurants, below) are delicious. But for the best deal, go to Falafel Dan (Ferdinand Bolstraat 126, 676-3411). During their "happy hours" from 15 to 17:00, there's an all-you-can-eat salad bar with unlimited falafel balls for only €3. Burp!

The quality and origin of the meat is a little dubious, but for **shoarma** take-aways try the Damstraat (just east of Dam Square), where there's a whole row of places. Prices start at about €3 to €4. Make sure you specify "small" if that's what you want or they'll try to give you a large and embarrass you into paying for it.

For **french fries** ("chips" to you Brits) try any place that advertises *vlaamse frites* (Flemish fries). These are the best. There's a large choice of toppings, but get mayonnaise for the Dutch experience. The best place, as evidenced by the long line-ups, is at Voetboogstraat 33, which runs parallel to the Kalverstraat. They're open daily until 18:00 (thurs 'til 19). There's also one at Damrak 42, just up from Central Station. And there's a pretty good one called De Belg at Reguliersbreestraat 49. A small is usually €1.40, plus €.35 each for a big selection of sauces. And, finally, if you don't mind spending a bit more, you can get fries made from organic potatoes at Dolores (see Restaurants, below). Delicious.

Healthy fast food is almost unheard of in Amsterdam, so this place is a find. Shakies (Central Station - west tunnel; 636-9836) makes great **juices and shakes**. All the fruit is freshly squeezed and the milk and yoghurt are organic. If you're vegan or lactose intollerent, they even have soyamilk. Prices start at €2.20 and for an extra €.60 they'll throw in a shot of vitamin B, ginseng, or guarana. Also on the menu are organic veggie samosas and tofu rolls (€2.10), bagels with cream cheese (€2.50), and herbal teas. Not bad for a food outlet in a train station. Open: mon-fri 7-21; sat 8:30-20:30; sun 9:30-20.

Loekie (Prinsengracht 705 at Leidsestraat; 624-4230) is a small deli that makes big, filling **sandwiches** on delicious, fresh-baked breads. Prices range from €2.50 to €5, and they'll build whatever you want from their huge selection of cheeses, patés, fish, and meat. They only do take-out, so get one and eat it by the canal.

Fish lovers should definitely try snacking at one of the herring stalls that are all over the city. They're easily recognizable by their fish flags. All kinds of **fish and seafood** sandwiches are available from €1.80. There's one close to Central Station on the bridge where the Haarlemmerstraat crosses the Singel canal and another next to the Westerkerk. Or for authentic British - read "deliciously greasy" - fish and chips, try Al's at Nieuwendijk 10.

Another good bet for cheap food is **Indonesian or Surinamese** take-away. A big roti meal will cost you about €3.50 to €4.50. A large plate of fried rice (nasi) or noodles (bami) with vegetables is about €4, and is often enough for two people. Add a couple of euros if you want it with chicken or pork. See Restaurants, below, for some suggestions.

For relatively cheap **Chinese** take-away look around the Zeedijk (off of Nieuwmarkt) where there's a small Chinatown. And at the markets don't forget to try the cheap and addictive Vietnamese *Loempias* (spring rolls): veggie or chicken, €.75.

The bakers at Mediteranee (Haarlemmersdijk 182) make delicious pastries and sweet-dough pizzas. But what they're really famous for are wonderful (vegan!) **croissants.** Buy four and get the fifth one free.

I'm not crazy about the other baked goods on offer at De Bakkerswinkel (Warmoesstraat 69), but the **scones** rock! Get there early though, they don't last long.

Febo is the name of a chain of gross automats that you'll see all over the city. Here you can get **greasy**, deep-fried snacks for about one euro. If you have to do it, your best bet is probably the *kaas* (cheese) soufflé. Here are a few locations: Damrak 6 (just down from Central Station); Kalverstraat 142; Nieuwendijk 220. They're open every night 'til 3:00.

Pizza slices in Amsterdam were my idea, damn it, and now they're everywhere. When they're fresh, New York Pizza (Leidsestraat 23; Spui 2; Damstraat 24) has the best slices in town. Prices range from €2.05 to €2.75. A big, doughy garlic bread with cheese is €2.35. Sbarro (Damrak 60) isn't bad either - which tells you how bad things really are.

night shops

"Night Shops" are the only places to buy groceries after the supermarkets close and are accordingly expensive. Fruit and veggies at these shops are a rip-off, but all the usual junk foods are available. Most night shops are open daily from 16 to 1:00. After that, you're fucked. Here are a few in the centre.

Pinguin Nightshop - Berenstraat 5

Between the Prinsengracht and the Keizersgracht. (Map area C5)

Big Bananas - Leidsestraat 73

This night shop does a lot of business because of its location, but what a grumpy bunch. (Map area C6)

Avondmarkt - de Wittenkade 94-96

The best selection and prices, but it's not in the centre. West end. (Map area B2)

Sterk - Waterlooplein 241

This place has cold-cuts, salads and cheeses too. (Map area E6)

Baltus T - Vijzelstraat 127

Between Prinsengracht and Weteringschans. (Map area D7)

Dolf - Willemsstraat 79

In the Jordaan. (Map area C2)

Texaco - Sarphatistraat 225; Marnixstraat 250

Open 24 hours. Eat here and get gas. (Map areas H6, B5)

all night eating

De Prins - Weteringschans 1

Conveniently situated right across the street from the Paradiso (see Music chapter), for your after-concert-french-fry craving. Open: sun-thurs 'til 3; fri/sat 'til 4. (Map area C7)

Surinam Express - Halvemansteeg 18

They cook up pretty good rice and noodle dishes late at night in this tiny joint. A full meal costs about €5, but if you're just peckish they have sandwiches from €2.25, and snacks from €1. There are only a few stools though, so it's pretty much eat and run. (Map area D6)

Bojo - Lange Leidsedwarsstraat 51

This Indonesian restaurant is a good place for a late night pig-out (see Restaurants, below). Open: sun-thurs 'til 2; fri/sat 'til 4. (Map area C7)

Gary's Late Nite - Reguliersdwarsstraat 53, 420-2406

Visit this little shop (see Cafés chapter), in the wee hours for muffins, cookies, and bagels. Open: sun-thurs 'til 3; fri/sat 'til 4. (Map area D6)

Dolores - Nieuwezijds Voorburgwal (opposite 289), 620-3302

In the summer, you can eat organic burgers and fries here in the middle of the night (see Restaurants, below). Open: (in summer) thurs 'til 1; fri/sat 'til 3. (Map Area D5)

easyEverything - Reguliersbreestraat 22

There's not a big selection of eats - brownies, packaged sandwiches, microwaved stuff - at this internet café (see Hanging Out chapter), but in the middle of the night in Amsterdam, you can't be too choosy. Open: daily 24 hours. (Map area D6)

Jerusalem - Haarlemmerstraat 117, 639-3007

Delicious (vegan!) croissants made by the baker at Mediterranee (see Street Foods, above). They also sell other pastries and warm meals, too. Open: sun-thurs 'til 1; fri/sat 'til 3. (Map area D3)

Febo Snackbars - all over

I can't really recommend this shit, but they're open late and they're cheap (see Street Food, above). Do what you gotta do. Open: daily 'til 3.

New York Pizza - Leidsestraat 23, Damstraat 24

Pizza slices until late (see Street Food, above). Open: sun-thurs 'til 1; fri/sat 'til 4. (Map area C6, D5)

bread

Le Marché - Kalverstraat 201; Rokin 160

Despite the crowds (which can be daunting), I frequently stop in here to pick up one of their delicious fresh breads: multi-grain, multi-seed, or garlic/thyme, to name but a few. They also bake panini, focaccia, an assortment of rolls, and they have ready-made sandwiches. It's some of the best bread in town. Open: mon-sat 10-19 (thurs 'til 21); sun 12-18. (Map area D6)

Bakker Wieteke - Plantage Doklaan 8-12

Once a week, this squat fills with the delicious smell of fresh bread. Also on offer are pizzas, cookies, and other baked goods, all made with organic ingredients. What's available changes from week to week and the quality is a bit hit-and-miss. There may be exquisite pear tarts waiting for you, or you might find that all that's left are some burnt vegan brownies. But the atmosphere is always pleasant, and there are a couple of little candle-lit tables set up for those who want to have something there with a cup of tea or organic wine. When you enter the building, the bakery is through the first door on the left. Open: wed 16-20. (Map area F6)

Bakery Paul Anée - Runstraat 25, 623-5322; Bellamystraat 2, 618-3113

Exclusively hearty, healthy items are sold at this famous bakery. I know people who are addicted to their muesli rolls. They also sell almond and cashew butter. Open: mon-fri 9-18; sat 9-17. (Map area C5)

free samples

I don't know how desperate you are but..

Stalls at the Organic Farmers' Market (see Shopping chapter) are a great source of free samples. Some Albert Heijn supermarkets have free coffee - usually by the deli counter. Bertolli Toscaans Lunchroom (Leidsestraat 54) has baskets of bread and a variety of olive oils to sample. Gary's Muffin's (see Cafés chapter) sometimes have one or two baskets on the counter with samples of their goodies. Ben & Jerry's (Leidsestraat 90; Kinkerstraat 142; platform 2 in Central Station) give away all the free ice cream you can eat on their free cone day (usually late April - check the *Get Lost!* website). And finally, it's not food, but the Body Shop (Kalverstraat 157) displays tester bottles of all their lotions, creams and perfumes. Just because you're travelling doesn't mean you should let yourself go.

breakfast

Breakfast is such a good meal, but if you're travelling on a budget you don't want to be forking out a lot of dough - especially so early in the day. If your hotel doesn't include breakfast, then here is a selection of eating spots where you can get something for less than €10.

For the record, an *uitsmijter* (pronounced "outsmyter") means bouncer, and it's what you serve your guests late at night just before you kick them out of your flat. It consists of an egg fried with cheese, ham or another meat and slipped onto a piece of toast. It's very Dutch.

Cafe Latei - Zeedijk 143, 625-7485

One of my favourite cafés (see Cafés chapter) has a breakfast special for €6.40 that includes coffee or tea, orange juice, a croissant, and a cheese sandwich. They also make uitsmijters and omelettes starting at €3.60, which means you can have one with a coffee and get out for less than €5. Open: mon-fri 8-17; sat 9-18; sun 11-18. (Map area E4)

Winkel Lunchcafé - Noordermarkt 43, 623-0223

If you're visiting one of the markets by the Noorderkerk on Saturday or Monday morning (see Markets, Shopping chapter) be sure to stop in at this very popular café on the corner of the square. They serve one of the best apple cakes in Amsterdam. Everyone gets a piece and sits outside drinking cappuccino or fresh orange juice at shared tables along the crowded Westerstraat. It costs €2.50 (€3 with whipped cream), but the slices are big and you'll feel stuffed. Open: mon 7-17; tues-fri 8-17; sat 7-18. (Map area C3)

Dimitri's Café - Prinsenstraat 3, 627-9393

Dimitri's is located on a very pretty street between two canals. It's a comfortable place to drink a pot of tea (€3) and read the paper while you wait for your breakfast. They've got yoghurt and muesli for €2.10, pancakes for €2.25, and until noon you can get a big breakfast for €6.25. If it's too crowded, try Vennington (Prinsenstraat 2; 625-9398), the little place across the street, which is also great. Open: daily 8-22. (Map area C3)

Lunchcafé Nielsen - Berenstraat 19, 330-6006

They serve a full breakfast here (see Restaurants, below) for €7.50, or if you want à la carte, they've got yoghurt, fruit salads, croissants, and organic bacon. Open: tues-fri 8-17; sat 8-18; sun 9-17. (Map Area C5)

De Peper - Overtoom 301, 779-4912

If you have a wild Saturday night and wake up late, plop yourself onto a couch at this squat restaurant (see below), listen to some tunes, and grab some brunch. Last time I was there they were serving a black-bean paté with a big salad, all made with organic produce. It wasn't gourmet, but it was only €3! Open: sun 12-17. (Map area A7)

Broodje Bert - Singel 321, 623-0382

This shop is tiny: just a few stools pushed up to a couple of counters that run along under the windows. For breakfast they've got the Ernie - coffee or tea, OJ, a croissant, french bread, jam, cheese, and ham for €5.50. Or the Bert - coffee or tea, OJ, eggs, bacon, and french bread for €6.50. Open: daily 8-17. (Map area C6)

Barney's Breakfast Bar - Haarlemmerstraat 102, 625-9761

And here's one for the wake and bake crowd: a coffeeshop that serves breakfast all day. Though the food is a bit pricey, many visitors appreciate being afforded the opportunity to simultaneously get wasted and chow down pancakes (€4.50), or a full breakfast (€6.70 to €8.70). The music is played a bit too loud, but it's a pleasant atmosphere nonetheless. Their sister bar just a few doors down has almost the same menu, but if you're a vegetarian keep to the coffeeshop where they maintain separate grills for animals and vegetables. Open: daily, 7-20 in summer; 8-20 in winter. (Map area D3)

Wintergarden (Hotel Krasnapolsky) - Dam 9, 554-9111

For a splurge, treat yourself to the breakfast buffet at the 19th century Wintergarden inside the Hotel Krasnapolsky, where you can eat your fill for €20. From the tiled floor, to the abundant plants and grand murals, to the wrought-iron balustrade and the glass roof almost 14 metres above you, it's spectacular. Open: daily 6:30-10:30. (Map area D4)

restaurants

Warung Mini - Ceintuurbaan 205, 662-6804

Surinamese/Indonesian. It's a bit out of the centre, but what a deal! Warung Mini serves up big, wonderful meals starting at only €4 for a vegetarian or chicken roti (curried veggies, egg, and a roti). There are also lots of rice and noodle dishes in the €5 to €6 range, soups for €2.75, and a choice of 20 different sandwiches for €2 to €2.50. Order at the counter, and they'll call you when it's ready. For dessert try "baked banana" - deep fried banana strips in a batter. Now that's what I'm talkin' about. Open: mon-sat 11-23; sun 12-23.

Albert Cuyp 67 - Albert Cuyp 67, 671-1396

Surinamese/Chinese. This little restaurant lies between two others that have basically the same menu, which in turn is similar to that of Warung Mini (above). Big portions for a low price, though sometimes a touch on the greasy side. They have a veggie or chicken roti for only €3.20! There are plenty of other choices for vegetarians too. The average price for a rice or noodle dish is about €5, and don't be shy to ask what's what. Excellent salted banana chips. Located near the Albert Cuyp market (see Markets, Shopping chapter). Open: daily 11-22.

Green Planet - Spuistraat 122, 625-8280

www.greenplanet.nl

Organic Vegetarian/Vegan. When you take into account the eco-friendliness of Green Planet - almost all of the ingredients in their homemade snacks and meals are organic, the electricity used in the restaurant is from green energy sources, and even their take-out packaging is biodegradable - the prices aren't as high as you might think. Their day menu, available from 11 to 16:00, consists of soups, salads, veggie burgers, and wraps. Prices run from about €5 to €10. Dinner is served from 18 to 22:30, with lovingly prepared dishes that average about €12.50. There are plenty of choices for vegans on the menu and, in fact, the chefs actually encourage special orders. For dessert try the classic English chocolate cake with whipped cream and fruit sauce. Mmm. Open: mon-sat 11-24. (Map area C4)

Vliegende Schotel (Flying Saucer) - Nieuwe Leliestraat 162, 625-2041

www.vliegendeschotel.com

Vegetarian. This restaurant is situated in a beautiful neighbourhood called the Jordaan (pronounced "yordahn"), so make sure that you take a walk around before or after your meal. They have a big menu that includes some vegan dishes. Meals start at €7.50 for their daily special, and run up to about €10.50. Half-servings are also available. Soup of the day is €2.80. Order at the back and leave your name. They'll run a tab for you and you pay as you leave. It's comfy and friendly inside, and the room on the left is non-smoking. The only problem here is that the service is very slow and they often run out of food. If you're in a hurry or are very hungry, make sure you show up early. Open: daily 16-23:30 (but the last call for dinner orders is at 22:15). (Map area B4)

Thais Snackbar Bird - Zeedijk 77, 420-6289

Thai. If you've ever been to Thailand you'll like this place. It's got the atmosphere down pat, with Thai pop songs, pictures of the king, and orchids on the tables. A lot of Thai people eat here, which is a good sign of authentic cooking. Meals aren't super cheap. They average about €8 (add a few euros if you want shrimp), but the food is always prepared fresh and it's delicious. Worth the walk through this sleazy, junkie-filled neighbourhood. Open: daily 15-22. (Map area E4)

Raan Phad Thai - Kloveniersburgwal 18, 420-0665

Thai. If Bird is too crowded, this friendly place is just a short walk up the street. There are only a few tables inside, under an old beamed ceiling, and the window offers a nice view of the canal. A salad is €3.50. Prices for main dishes range from €7 for a Thai curry with rice, to €12 for fried noodles with shrimp. Open: daily 13-21. (Map area E5)

Cook Kai - 2e Rozendwaarstraat 3, 528-7887

www.cookkai.nl

Thai. It seems like the best Thai restaurants in Amsterdam are all tiny. This one is really cute. It's on a little side street in the Jordaan and it only has room for 3 small tables next to their open kitchen. But the three women cooking here are not only friendly, but fast, so there's usually not too long a wait for a table. I've worked my way through most of their vegetarian offerings and they've all been excellent. Lately I keep coming back for number 83 - tofu with mixed veggies and Thai basil in a red coconut-curry sauce. Oh yeah! Prices start at €8.30 for a filling main dish, so you can get a meal and a drink for about €10. Figure in a couple more euros if you want meat. Open: daily 16-21:30. (Map area B5)

Kam Yin - Warmoesstraat 6, 625-3115

Surinamese/Chinese. The best food of this type (at the right price) in the centre of Amsterdam. They have a big take-away menu of rice and noodle items and the servings are huge. Dishes start as low as €4 and one main dish along with a side order is probably enough for two people. You can also eat-in for just a little bit more. Two minutes from Central Station. Open: daily 12-24. (Map area E4)

Lunchcafé Nielsen - Berenstraat 19, 330-6006

Western healthy. Before or after you finish exploring the charming little streets in this neighbourhood, stop by this lively, family-run cafe for a freshly prepared breakfast or lunch. But don't be in a rush: the tasty, reasonably priced food draws in a lot of people, and it's always busy. The menu is in English and has plenty of vegetarian choices, a few vegan, and the meat they do serve is free-range. A full breakfast is €7.50, or you can go à la carte if you just want a fruit salad or an omelet. They also have sandwiches from €3.30, bagels from €1.50, salads from €3.15, and homemade soups from €3. *Eet smaakelijk.* Open: tues-fri 8-17; sat 8-18; sun 9-17. (Map Area C5)

Foodism - Oude Leliestraat 8, 427-5103

Everything. This funky little restaurant is on the same pretty street as Grey Area (see Coffeeshops, Cannabis chapter). They make wonderful soups, salads, sandwiches, and a delicious vegetarian pasta. It's also a nice place to enjoy a leisurely brunch with some friends. Although it's open for dinner, I actually prefer it earlier in the day before it gets too smoky. Open: daily "around 10:30 'til 22:00". (Map area C4)

Dolores - Nieuwezijds Voorburgwal (opposite 289), 620-3302

Everything. Dolores has turned this cute historic cottage into one of the best snackbars in town. In her tiny kitchen she cooks up veggie burgers (€3.50), beef burgers, and fries (€2.50), all made from organic ingredients. There are lots of other organic items on the menu too, some of them suitable for vegans. Fish eaters should try the Red Snapper sandwich (€6) or the crab cakes (€4), which are very popular. It's not the cheapest place, but the food is healthy and flavourful. Inside there's only room for a few people to eat sitting on stools, but as long as the weather's nice there are a couple of tables outside, too. Open: monsat 11-20 (thurs 'til 22); sun 12-20; in summer, thurs 'til 01; fri/sat 'til 03. (Map Area D5)

Maoz Falafel - Reguliersbreestraat 45, 624-9290; Muntplein 1, 420-7435

www.maoz.nl

Falafel. Delicious, freshly made falafel balls are served here in a warm pita for only €3.50 (€2.50 for a small). Then you cram as much stuff from the salad-and-sauce bar as you can into the pita, adding more as you eat. It's one of the cheapest meals in town. Maoz has started franchising, so you'll find them all over, but I think the best outlets are the original take-away stall near the Rembrandtplein or, if you want to sit down, the corner shop looking over the Muntplein. Stop by after a movie in the Tuschinski (see Film chapter). Reguliersbreestraat open: daily, in summer, 11-4; in winter 11-1. Muntplein open: daily, in summer 11-2; in winter 11-1. (Map area D6)

De Peper - Overtoom 301, 779-4912

www.contrast.org/peper

Organic Vegan. After sitting empty for some time, this former film school was squatted. It now houses several studios, a movie theatre (see Film chapter) living spaces, and a great restaurant called De Peper. It's very popular so make sure you call at 16:00 to reserve a meal. Let them know when you arrive, and then kick back with a beer or juice. Everything on offer is organic - even the cognac! Food is served at 19:00 and the meal consists of a starter (usually soup) and a lovingly prepared main course. The €5 price is cheap for healthy, vegan food. Dessert costs an extra €1.20. They cook three nights a week. The bar stays open late (and is also open on Thursday night from 21:00) and sometimes there are parties and performances after dinner. From Leidseplein it's about a 10 minute walk, or you can hop on tram 1. Open: tues, fri, sun 18-23. (Map area A7)

Addis Ababa - Overtoom 337, 618-4472

www.addisababa.nl

Ethiopian. This is a great restaurant to go to with a bunch of friends. The food is served in the traditional way, on a giant platter, and everyone eats with their hands. The decor is lively and the owner is a really nice guy. They serve several veggie dishes, and something for carnivores, too. A full meal and a drink (try the banana beer!) will set you back about €10 to €12 per person. Open: daily 17-23. (Map area A7)

Soup En Zo - Jodenbreestraat 94a, 422-2243

www.soupenzo.nl

Soup. In a welcome addition to Amsterdam's culinary scene, the concept of the soup stall has arrived. The cooks in this little restaurant use fresh, often organically grown, vegetables in their soups. And there are always several vegetarian options. It's not super cheap (averaging €2.50 to €5.50 for a bowl), but the soups really are delicious, and in nice weather there are tables out front. They also serve salads and Brazilian fruit shakes. Soup en Zo is located close to the Waterlooplein market. They have another shop at Nieuwe Spiegelstraat 54, but you can only get take-away. Jodenbreestraat location open: mon-sat 12-19; sun 13-19. (Map area E6)

Bar Soup - Govert Flinckstraat 153, 673-0006

www.barsoup.nl

Soup. This sweet, relaxed little shop rests on a quiet street in the Pijp neighbourhood (pronounced "pipe"), just around the corner from the Albert Cuyp Market (see Markets, Shopping). Five different freshly made soups are on offer each day, and they're all excellent. Ask for a little taste if you can't make up your mind. The soups cost anywhere from €2.40 to €6.70, depending on the size, and they're served with a big hunk of delicious bread. Salads and quiche are also made here - try the wild spinach and mushroom (€3). For dessert, there's homemade chocolate mousse (€2.50), carrot cake, brownies, and more. It's a popular place so expect to share a table. Enjoy. Open: mon-fri 11:30-22; sat 12:30-21; sun 14-22.

La Place Grand Café Restaurant - Kalverstraat 201, Rokin 160, 622-0171
www.laplace.nl

Everything. Occupying a couple of little seventeenth-century houses, this department store food court lacks the usual fast-food crap and atmosphere. Elegant little booths display a wide variety of beautiful fresh fruits and vegetables bought directly from the producers. The menu changes daily and everything is prepared fresh. Here are some of the cheaper examples from the last time I was here: sandwiches, €2.29; soup, €2.79; excellent french fries, €1.89; giant hot chocolate with whipped cream, €1.89. There are also a couple of salad bars - fruit (€2.79) and vegetable (€3.29) - where you can test your architectural skills by piling on as much as will fit on a plate. Upstairs, there's a non-smoking section, and if the weather is nice there's a small balcony over the Kalverstraat that's great for people-watching. The bakery attached to this restaurant makes some of the best bread in Amsterdam. Open: mon 11-20; tues-sat 10-20 (thurs 'til 21); sun 12-20. (Map area D6)

Du Shue Fang - Zeedijk 118, 420-2357

Vegetarian Chinese. Tucked away in the bottom left corner of the He Hwa Buddhist temple, unnoticed by most of the passing crowd, is a simple, little restaurant serving vegetarian Chinese food. Everything on the menu is priced at €2.50, which is a good deal for the small bowls of rice and noodles, and not so good for the fresh-squeezed juice. But unlike most restaurants in Amsterdam, they will give you extra water for your tea without charging you. While one dish and a drink isn't really filling, it does make for a tasty light lunch in a clean, minimalist environment strikingly at odds with the craziness of the district outside. Open: mon-fri 12-20. (Map area E4)

Dim Sum Court - Zeedijk 109, 638-1466; Rokin 52, 638-1249

All-you-can-eat Chinese. Okay, the food is crap, and the best thing about this place is the sign out front, but if you're super hungry and really want to pig out, then €7.50 (or closer to €10 with the compulsory drink) gets you 60 minutes of shovelling time. Open: daily 12-23. (Map area E4; D6)

Zaal 100 - De Wittenstraat 100, 688-0127
www.wittereus.net/zaal100.html

Vegetarian/vegan. There are all kinds of cultural events going on in this building (which was squatted in 1984), but to find the food, go in the main doors and turn to your right. The first door on your right, just past the bar, is the one you want. Inside is a crowded, cosy room filled with tables and mismatched chairs. There are stairs in the hallway that lead up to a small balcony with more seating. It's perfectly acceptable to share a table if the place is busy. A full meal of soup, a big plate of food for the main dish, and dessert, will usually only run you about €5. It's not a gourmet meal, but it is tasty and filling. You don't need to reserve, but you should show up early. Wednesdays are vegan. Closed in July and August. Open: tues, wed 18-20. (Map area B2)

Einde van de Wereld (End of the World) - Javakade (opposite #21), Java Island

Home-cooked. Some years back, with a lot of hard work by volunteers, the lively atmosphere of this famous squat restaurant was transplanted onto a boat! Step down into the hold of the ship and there's a bright, bustling room filled with great music and the smell of home cooking. Go early as they only serve until the food runs out. There's a choice of a vegetarian (€5.50) or an organic meat dish (€7.50) or a half plate (lots of kids here). Dessert costs €2. Though the deliciousness quotient varies, it's always a good deal: the servings are huge and there's also bread and garlic butter on the tables. Drinks are cheap. Order your meal at the bar, leave your name, pay, and in about 15 minutes they'll bring you your food. In good weather, take your beer and sit up top, overlooking the water. The boat's name is *Quo Vadis* and there's little sign in front. You can take bus 32 from Central Station eastbound (it'll say "KNSM Eiland" on the front), to the Javakade stop. Then follow the road to the left for a few minutes. Or better yet, take a bicycle so you can cruise around a bit before or after your meal: the interesting architecture in this newly built neighbourhood is world-renowned. AMP is also in this area (see Live Music/Party Venues, Music chapter). Einde van de Wereld is open only on Wednesdays and Fridays from 18:00. (Map area I3)

Toscana - Haarlemmerstraat 130, 622-0353; Haarlemmerdijk 176, 624-8358

Italian. I'm always complaining to visitors about how pathetic Amsterdam pizzas are. And this place is no exception. But, all their pizzas are half price and I love a bargain. The cheapest pizza is a thin, but big, margherita for €4.55, which means you can have a pizza and a beer for about €6.50. And even though I bitch a fair bit, it's not terrible pizza. "When the moon hits your eye, like a big pizza pie, that's *amoré*..." Open: daily 16-23. (Map area C2)

Pannekoekhuis Upstairs - Grimburgwal 2, 626-5603

Pancakes. Not having a pancake in Holland would be like coming here and not seeing a windmill. It's part of the Dutch experience. This tiny place is on the second floor of a very cute, very old house. Prices start at €4.50 for a powdered sugar topping. A pancake with strawberries and whipped cream goes for €5.15; banana with chocolate sauce is €6.50; and a pot of tea costs €2. Open: mon-fri 12-19; sat 12-18; sun 12-17. Closed in January. (Map area D5)

Bojo - Lange Leidsedwarsstraat 51, 626-8990 (694-2864 for hotel delivery)

www.bojo.nl

Indonesian. This place is in all the tourist guides, but a lot of Dutch people go here too because whatever the food lacks in excitement is made up for with huge servings and reasonable prices (€6 and up). And they're open late. Skip the appetizers: they're not very good. The entrees are pretty good, but if you want a real Indonesian "rice table" (and they're excellent) you have to pay at least €20 per person. If you have the dough try "Cilubang" (Runstraat 10; 626-9755) where the food is fantastic. Bojo is open: mon-thurs 16-2; fri 16-4; sat 12-4; sun 12-2. (Map area C7)

Keuken van 1870 - Spuistraat 4, 624 8965

Cafeteria food. It opened as a soup kitchen in 1870, and you can still get a very cheap, basic meal here. Full course, meat-and-potato dishes go for about €5.50. It's close to Central Station. Open: mon-fri 12-20; sat 16-21. (Map area D3)

MKZ - Eerste Schinkelstraat 16, 679-0712

Vegan/Vegetarian. MKZ is an abbreviation of the Dutch words for hoof-and-mouth disease, so it's no surprise that the only things slaughtered here for your eating pleasure are vegetables. Big plates of healthy food are dished up 3 nights a week by volunteer crews that change each evening. For a while, the *Koken met Tieten* (Cooks with Tits) nights - when the mostly female chefs worked topless - were very popular. The restaurant is in a great space at the edge of the squatted Binnenpret complex. You might want to combine a meal here with a visit to the sauna (see Saunas, Hanging Out chapter), or a concert at OCCII (see Music chapter). In the summer you can eat out in the courtyard, but in winter it can get very chilly so try to snag a seat near the heater or the open kitchen. The last time I was here, soup and a main dish was only €3.50, and dessert was an extra €.50. Drinks are super cheap, too: juice and tea €.50; wine or a bottle of beer €1! Call in the afternoon to reserve. Food is served at 19.00. Open: tues - thurs.

The Fridge - Frederick Hendrikstraat 111, 684-6437

Vegetarian. With the beats of different DJs to inspire them, the organizers of this very cool restaurant whip up delicious, healthy food two nights a week. The filling dinners cost €7 on Wednesday, and a little more on Thursday when all the ingredients are organic. They start with soup (which the cooks are particularly good at concocting). Then a main dish is served and later, a dessert. There's no menu - if they feel like cooking Japanese, or Indian, or Mexican, then that's what they cook. You never know until you get there. The bar stays open after the meal if you want to hang out for awhile and listen to the tunes. Open: wed/thurs 18-21. (Map area A4)

Fine dining at the Fridge

Café de Molli - Van Ostadestraat 55, 676-1427

Vegetarian/Vegan. This place serves up cheap, big meals every Tuesday evening. Just €3 gets you a full veggie or vegan meal in a very basic, communal setting. Call the number above in the afternoon to reserve your meal. For a little more info about this squat see the Cafés chapter. Meals are served at 19:00.

The Atrium - Oudezijds Achterburgwal 237, 525-3999

Cafeteria food. This is a self-service student mensa with cheap meals. Outside of meal times it's also a pleasant place to grab an inexpensive cup of coffee and a croissant and to rest your feet a bit. Meals are served on weekdays from 12 to 14:00 and 17 to 19:30. There's another student mensa, Agora, at Roetersstraat 13, that also offers cheap meals and has a big non-smoking section. Same hours as the Atrium. (Map area D5)

Hap-Hmm - 1e Helmersstraat 33, 618-1884

www.welcome.to/hap-hmm

Dutch food. Just like dinner in mom's kitchen. Hap-Hmm is a little eatery located on a residential street that runs parallel to the Overtoom. They serve a lot of meat dishes, but there's also always a selection of vegetables, and lately they've been adding different sorts of veggie and tofu burgers to the menu, too. The set menus start at €5, salads go for €1.75, and soup-of-the-day is €1.25. It's nothing fancy, but it's a good price for a filling Dutch meal in a homey environment. Expect the other diners to be old folk from the neighbourhood, and other people with *Get Lost!*. Open: mon-fri 16:30-20. (Map area 7B)

Moeder's Pot - Vinkenstraat 119, 623-7643

Dutch food. It may be called Mother's Pot, but it's really Pop's Grill. Except for the kitchen, Pop hasn't fixed the place up in a long time, and it has an atmosphere of neglect. The food, however, is tasty and plentiful. Generous servings of authentic Dutch meat-and-potato dishes can be had for less than €5. A vegetable omelette is €4.30. The vegetable plate (*not* suitable for vegetarians) is a great deal at €3.60, especially if you're tired and hungry after a long day. Open: mon-fri 17-22; sat 17-21:30. (Map area C2)

Restaurant de Hemelvaart - Oude Haagseweg 58, 06-48375025

www.rijkshemelvaart.com

Vegetarian. Way the hell out by the Amsterdamse Bos (see Parks, Hanging Out chapter), in an old military compound that was squatted in 1989, a small group of people have created a "free state" in which to live and work. One of the several projects going on at the site is a vegetarian restaurant that's open most summers (and now and then in the winter) in one form or another. In the past they've combined meals with DJs, films, and video re-runs of *The Love Boat*. The generous servings of whatever food they cook up, usually soup, a main dish, and dessert (the menu is sometimes online) costs about €8. Drinks are cheap, too. If the weather is good, you can eat outside. Call first to make sure they're open and to make a reservation. Then make a day of it by riding out to the Bos before you eat. Otherwise you can take tram 2 to the second last stop, after which it's about a 10-minute walk. Open Saturdays in the summer from 18:30.

Special Bite

www.specialbite.com

Want more restaurant suggestions? For an extensive, independent listing of Amsterdam's restaurants in all price ranges, try *Special Bite*. They have an excellent website that's updated regularly, and a printed guide that appears quarterly. Both are in English, easy to use, and fun to read.

Cafés

Cafés are plentiful in Amsterdam, and they're ideal places to hang out and get a feel for the city. Once you've ordered you'll be left alone to read or write postcards or vegetate for as long as you like. Don't be shy to ask to share a table if you see a free chair: this is one of the most densely populated countries in the world (16 million people) and table sharing is customary.

There's been a minor revolution on the coffee scene in Amsterdam. Only a couple of years ago, you could visit a dozen cafés before your request for a cup of decaf would be met with much more than a blank stare; if you asked for an "ordinary coffee" you'd almost invariably be served a watered-down espresso; and a cup of joe "to go" was virtually unheard of. Now you can find any of these delights on almost every block in the centre.

Koffie verkeerd (literally "incorrect coffee") is café au lait. Tea is charged by the cup and extra water will be added to your bill. I don't know the reason for this dumb custom. Fresh-squeezed orange juice, which is commonly referred to in french - *jus d'orange* - is available in most cafés.

Many cafés also serve snacks such as *broodjes* (small sandwiches) and tostis (usually ham and/or cheese sandwiches squashed into a sandwich toaster). Prices start at about €2 for a plain cheese-on-white-roll or *tosti*. Another popular item is apple cake with whipped cream. It's an incredibly delicious Amsterdam speciality that should definitely be experienced.

Tobacco warning: many Dutch people think nothing of lighting up during a meal and blowing the smoke in your face. It's disgusting and unpleasant, but for the time-being, it's the norm here.

For internet cafés, see the Hanging Out chapter.

Café Latei - Zeedijk 143, 625-7485

Do you ever wake up and think to yourself, "I feel like drinking a cup of coffee, then buying some organic olive oil and a piece of furniture"? Because this cute, split-level café's got all that and more. Almost everything in here is for sale: the chair you're sitting on, Finnish wallpaper, knick-knacks, and a variety of olive oils. The way everything is scattered about here creates the sensation that you're in someone's living room. It's a great little place to pop into for a fresh-squeezed juice and a big bowl of soup, or a sandwich made with organic bread. Open: mon-fri 8-17; sat 9-18; sun 11-18. (Map area E4)

Villa Zeezicht - Torensteeg 7, 626-7433

Even with their expansion into the shop next door, this remains a cosy café. The seats by the big windows are perfect for reading the paper and people-watching. In the summer there are tables outside and on the bridge across the street. Sandwiches start at €2.75. They also make an awesome apple cake for €2.50 (a meal in itself). Make sure to ask for whipped cream (€.75). Open: mon-fri 8-21; sat/sun 9-21. (Map area D4)

Café ter Kuile - Torensteeg 8, 639-1055

This pretty café/bar gets very crowded in the day with students from the university. But at night, after the dinner hour, it becomes mellower. I'm talking candles on the table, Tom Waits on the stereo, and a warm buzz of conversation. It's a good place to shoot the shit with a friend. Open: daily 11-1; fri/sat 'til 3. (Map area D4)

Backstage Boutique and Coffee-Corner

Utrechtsedwarsstraat 67, 622-3638

Greg, one of the Christmas Twins (identical twins who were big stars back in the US), died a few years ago, and he is missed by many, many people. But his brother Gary is still running the Peewee-esque café they built together, and its unique atmosphere endures. It's not really cheap, but this place is great! They serve coffees, teas, juices and an assortment of sandwiches and cakes. The bottom of the menu proclaims: "Mama wanted girls!" The walls are decorated with wild sweaters and hats that were designed and made by the twins. If you're lucky, you might even walk out with a souvenir postcard. Gary is super friendly and very funny. Open: mon-sat 10-18. (Map area E7)

Café Vertigo - Vondelpark 3, 612-3021

www.vertigo.nl

This café has one of the nicest (and busiest) terraces in Amsterdam. It's located in the middle of Vondelpark in the Film Museum building (see Film chapter). In bad weather duck into the cosy, low-ceilinged café. On Saturday nights they have DJs. Sometimes there are slide shows at the back. Open: daily 11-1 (from 10 in spring and summer). (Map area B8)

Tofani - Kloveniersburgwal 20

There's nothing pretentious about this Italian shop near the Nieuwmarkt. It's an old-school joint selling great sandwiches and wonderful gelato. Five different sandwiches are served on panini bread. A mozzarella, lettuce, tomato and basil goes for €3.50. There are also hot sandwiches. Order at the counter and have a seat at one of the tables outside. They'll tap on the window when it's ready. It's perfect for a fast lunch, especially when the weather is nice. Open: mar-oct only. (Map area E5)

The Coffee Gallery - Jodenbreestraat 94, 06-535-25929

www.coffeegallery.nl

With it's two small tables and a few stools by the window, this petite café is another that brings a little bit of Italy to Amsterdam. The panini sandwiches here are lovingly made. A vegetariano is only €2.50. For a bit more you can add some prosciutto. If it's too busy, you can always get a soup next door at Soup En Zo (see Restaurants, Food chapter) and then come here for a cappuccino and some delicious gelato (€.80 a scoop). Or get one of their top-quality coffees to go for only €1. Open: in summer, mon-sat 8:30-18, sun 12-18; in winter, mon-sat 8:30-18. (Map area E6)

De Tuin - 2e Tuindwarsstraat 13, 624-4559

De Tuin is a spacious, inviting café right in the heart of a beautiful old neighbourhood called the Jordaan. It's a traditional "brown café" (so-called because of the abundance of wood). I like to explore the area and then pop in here for drink and a sandwich. There are usually cool people hanging out and it's a comfortable spot to relax for awhile. The view of the Westerkerk tower from this shopping street is particularly photogenic. Open: mon-thurs 10-1; fri/sat 10-2; sun 11-1. (Map area B3)

Café de Pels - Huidenstraat 25, 622-9037

This is another traditional "brown café" with a diverse clientele. It's warm and welcoming in the winter, while in the summer the tiny outdoor tables make for good people-watching on this quaint little street. It has an authentic Amsterdam ambiance. Open: sun-thurs 10-1; fri/sat 10-3. (Map area C5)

Bagels & Beans - Ferdinand Bolstraat 70, 672-1610; Keisersgracht 504; Van Baerlestraat 40
www.bagelsbeans.nl

The bagels here, for my money, are the best in Amsterdam. They're often served hot out of the oven. A bagel with cream cheese costs €2.60. They serve delicious coffees too. But I can't handle the thick tobacco smoke that engulfs everything, so I usually get something to go, or I head for their newest shop on the Van Baerlestraat which has a pretty garden out back. Open: mon-fri 8:30-18; sat 9:30-18; sun 10-18:00.

Gary's Muffins - Prinsengracht 454; Reguliersdwarsstr 53; Jodenbreestr 15; Raadhuisstr 18
www.garys-muffins.nl

Though I'm not crazy about Gary's baked goods, I still stop in sometimes for a a bagel with cream cheese (€2,50) and a cup of organic, fair-trade coffee. Organic muesli and yoghurt (€2.65) is also on the menu. Usually you can pick up day-old muffins and cookies for €.80. The Prinsengracht and Jodenbreestraat locations have tables outside in the summer. Gary's Late Night on Reguliersdwarstraat is open during the day, but I often swing by when I've got the munchies in the middle of the night. Open: daily 9-17:30. Gary's Late Night is open: sun-thurs 12-3; fri/sat 12-4.

De Ruimte - Eerste Constantijn Huygenstraat 20, 427-5951
www.smartprojectspace.net

The Smart Project Space was created by a network of artists to enable and promote contemporary (particularly new-media) art. While debate over the future of the building continues, it'll be used for exhibitions, films (see Film chapter), and other activities. The café/restaurant De Ruimte is part of the project. During the day the atmosphere in the café is hip, yet super-mellow. Drinks aren't cheap, but I like to drop in here to kick back for a bit and listen to some jazzy beats before wandering through the exhibition space. At night, a trendy crowd usually fills the restaurant. Open: tues-sun, midday-late. (Map area A7)

Lunchlokaal Wynand Fockink - Pijlsteeg 31, 639-2695

The quaint little courtyard where this café is located provides respite from the flurry of the Dam Square area. It's only open in the summer, when the trees and plants grow lush around the little tables, creating a wonderfully peaceful environment. It's not super cheap, but they have sandwiches from €4, and soup of the day with bread for €5. Go through the covered walkway by Leonida's chocolates on Damstraat and you'll find it. Open: daily, April to the end of September, 10-19. (Map area D5)

Café de Molli - Van Ostadestraat 55, 676-1427

This is a volunteer-run squat café with an emphasis on politics. They frequently host theme nights with videos and speakers on subjects such as genetically modified food, or the role of Shell (those murdering motherfuckers) in Nigeria. On Tuesday nights at 19:00 they serve super-cheap meals (see Restaurants, Food chapter). On other nights it's just a mellow place to hang out and meet some people. Drinks are very cheap. Tea is free. They also have a feminist café every second Wednesday of the month where a vegetarian meal is served. And Sundays are smoke-free. Open: mon 22-1; sun, tues-fri 21-1.

W139 - Warmoesstraat 139, 622-9434

www.W139.nl

This building was squatted back in 1979 and turned into an art gallery. The space is huge - perfect for the regularly changing, multi-media exhibitions on display. There's no charge to visit. The café, when it's open, is somewhat grungy, but cheap. They serve wine and malt beer as well as tea and coffee. Open: wed-sun 13-18:00. (Map area D4)

De Jaren - Nieuwe Doelenstraat 20, 625-5771

www.cafe-de-jaren.nl

I find the food overpriced here, but I like the spaciousness, which is unusual in this city and means that you can almost always find a seat. In the summer there are two big terraces with a terrific view over the Amstel River. It's right by the university and lots of intellectuals hang out here reading books. I often stop in to use the toilet. Located between Waterlooplein and Rembrandtplein. Open: sun-thurs 10-1; fri/ sat 10-2. (Map area D6)

Manege - Vondelstraat 140, 618-0942

I'd always heard that this horse riding school had a great café with cheap drinks and snacks. It's true. Vondelstraat runs alongside Vondelpark (see Parks, Hanging Out chapter). Walk through the arch under the huge lamps, and enter the school via the big doors. The café is through the door on the left, and up a grandiose stairway. There's a balcony with tables overlooking the training area, but if you find the horsey aroma a bit much, you can still see through the windows of the main room of the café. It was formerly very elegant and is now filled with cats. If you're coming from the park, take the exit near the Film Museum. Open: mon-fri 10-24; sat 10-17; sun 10-16. (Map area A7)

De Badcuyp - 1e Sweelinckstraat 10, 675-9669

www.badcuyp.demon.nl

This former bathhouse was saved from demolition by activists in the neighbourhood. Now it's a "centre for art, culture and politics" that's partly run by volunteers. It's located in the middle of the crowded Albert Cuyp Market (see Markets, Shopping chapter), and in nice weather there are tables outside. Inside it's spacious and relaxed: newspapers are scattered around and art exhibits line the walls. The upper level gives you a good view of the shoppers in the market below. They have a bar that serves cheap snacks from 11 to 15:00, and full meals in the evening (the daily special costs €7.50). There's often live music, either in the café or in the hall upstairs where they also host popular dance nights featuring salsa, funk, blues, jazz and disco. Open: tues-thurs 17-1; fri 17-3; sat 11-03; sun 17-1. (Map area E8)

East of Eden - Linnaeusstraat 11A, 665-0743

A spacious café right across the street from the Tropenmuseum (see Museum chapter). The seating is a mish-mash of couches and easy chairs and lots of light comes in through the high windows on two sides. It's warm and mellow and the only problem is that it gets very smoky. Non-smokers should visit this café in the summer when they have an outdoor terrace. Open: sun-thurs 11-1; fri/sat 11-2. (Map area H7)

De Roos (The Rose) - PC Hooftstraat 183 (entrance in Vondelpark), 689-5477

www.roos.nl

If you're into "creative and spiritual growth" or alternative health care, this centre might interest you. It's located at the edge of Vondelpark and is home to a new age shop, practitioners' rooms and a pretty tea room. From 12 to16:00 they offer a lunch menu that includes miso and other soups (€2 to €3.10), sandwiches (about €2), salads, and homemade cakes and pastries. Drinks are also low-priced, making it one of the best deals in this ritzy neighbourhood. On weekdays dinner is served from 17:30 to 20:00. Order downstairs and then take your tray up to the plant-filled solarium where classical music plays from the adjacent shop. Check the bulletin board for info about events in the community or talk to the staff at the reception desk. Tea room open: mon-fri 9-22; sat/sun 9-17. (Map area B7)

De Engel (The Angel) - Albert Cuypstraat 182, 675-0544

www.de-engel.net

The arms of the golden angel perched on the roof of this former church beckon you from the crowds of the Albert Cuypmarkt (see Markets Shopping chapter), and into a spacious interior that's reminiscent of an old colonial cafe. In fact, most of the furnishings were gleaned from aged buildings as far afield as France, the U.S. and Egypt. It's beautiful, especially the giant hanging lamps, which are an extraordinary sight. I've never eaten here, but during the day they have soup (€3.60), and sandwiches that are just a bit pricier than other cafes in the neighbourhood. I just like stopping in for a fresh orange juice (€2.20), or coffee (which is a bit cheaper at the bar). On Sundays they host breakfast concerts, with classical or jazz music and a full breakfast for €8.50. Open: sun-thurs 10-1; fri/sat 10-2.

OBA (Amsterdam Public Library) - Prinsengracht 587, 523-0900

Turn left through the front doors of the central library (see Hanging Out chapter) and you'll find their cafe. It's a little run-down, and not particularly pleasant, but it is cheap. A small, fresh, healthy sandwich and a fresh-squeezed orange juice will run you just €3. Soup of the day is €1.50. Coffee is €1, tea is only €.75, and re-fills are cheaper. A friendly red tabby cat makes its home here amongst all the newspapers, many of which are in English. Don't go out of your way, but if you're on a budget and in the neighbourhood, it's a good place to re-fuel. Open: mon 13-21; tues-thurs 10-21; fri/sat 10-17; sun (oct-mar) 13-17. (Map area B6)

Café Américain - Leidseplein 28, 556-3000

Gorgeous stained-glass lamps hang from vaulted ceilings. Huge windows look out over the bustle of Leidseplein. Every exposed surface is elaborately ornamented. And soft leather couches and easy chairs invite you to lounge for awhile. The cafe in this Art Deco hotel (where Mata Hari once stayed) is beautiful. Expensive too, so I usually just order a cup of tea and enjoy the atmosphere. Open: sun-fri 7-23; sat 7-24. (Map area B7)

cannabis

I n Amsterdam, you can walk into any "coffeeshop" (a café selling grass and hash) and order a coffee and a joint; then sit back and smoke, listen to music, perhaps have a game of backgammon or chess - without the worry of being arrested. How civilized!

Almost all coffeeshops have a menu listing the types of smoke available and where each one is from. It's fun to try grass and hash from different parts of the world, but I have to say that a lot of the *nederwiet* (Dutch grown weed) is spectacular. Prices are usually listed by the gram, but often sold in set-price bags of €5 or €10. Some coffeeshops will let you buy smaller amounts, too. Don't be shy to ask to see the menu, it's there to make it easy for you. Some strains are listed as "hydro" meaning that it was grown hydroponically. Others are listed as "bio", meaning it was grown in soil. Note that "bio", in this case, doesn't mean that it was grown organically - as it does with bio products in grocery stores. However, many coffeeshops are starting to sell organically grown weed and may list these as bio too. If you're in doubt, just ask. It's also no problem to ask to see the buds before you pay. Then relax while you roll and ponder the absurdity of North America's repressive and hypocritical "war on drugs", and how fantastic it is to be in Amsterdam!

D-Monica

You don't have to buy weed every time you go into a coffeeshop, but definitely buy something: a drink or some munchies.

The weed here is probably a lot stronger than what you're used to back home. If you find that a friend of yours is too high or feels a bit sick, often a sweet drink (like a cola) will help. Just thought I'd mention that.

Attention: Don't buy anything on the street! You will definitely be ripped off!

Warning: Space cakes and bonbons (containing grass or hash) are sold in some coffeeshops. They can be very strong, almost like tripping, so have fun, but be prepared for a long, intense high. Also keep in mind that they can take up to a couple of hours to kick in, so don't gobble down another one just because you don't feel anything right away................................ What?

coffeeshops

Dampkring - Handboogstraat 29, 638-0705

www.dampkring.nl

The super-funky decor and some killer hash and buds have made the Dampkring a longtime favourite with locals and tourists alike. It can get pretty crowded in here, and if you're looking for a mellow experience the music can be a little loud, but otherwise it's a comfortable shop with friendly, knowledgeable staff. Their extensive menu (which they sell as a souvenir) details what type of high you can expect from the various strains and includes information on their "fair trade" policies as well. Fair trade cannabis! Only in Amsterdam. Open: mon-thurs 10-1; fri/sat 10-2; sun 11-1. (Map area C6)

Tweede Kamer - Heisteeg 6, 422-2236

This is a sweet little coffeeshop with the same great menu as the Dampkring. They renovated recently, and even though the space is small, the shop feels open and inviting. I've also found the staff to be patient and informative with tourists who needed a little time to make up their minds. That's cool. Open: mon-sat 10-1; sun 11-1. (Map area D5)

Amnesia - Herengracht 133, 638-3003

The new owners of Amnesia have transformed it into an excellent coffeeshop. The interior is stylish, comfortable, and not too smoky thanks to a giant new air filter. There's a good selection of top-notch weed and hash on the menu, some of it organically grown. And it's great to hear the likes of Curtis Mayfield and Miles Davis on the sound system when you're getting high. Add to all this a pinball machine and a view of the brothel traffic across the street, and you've got the makings of a very entertaining visit. Open: daily 9-1. (Map area C4)

Grey Area - Oude Leliestraat 2, 420-4301

www.greyarea.nl

Originally, this tiny coffeeshop was Amsterdam's first hempseed restaurant. Now they only serve tasty morsels of the smokable kind. They have a very select menu offering some of the newest strains of weed around, yet despite this exclusivity, their prices are very reasonable. Connoisseurs will definitely get a kick out of this place. Most of the time the staff are friendly and welcoming, and the organic coffee is served in a bottomless cup! Play the game on their website and you get a printable coupon you can bring with you for a free drink. Open: tues-sun 12-20. (Map area C4)

Global Chillage - Kerkstraat 51, 777-9777

www.globalchillage.com

It's not the happening place it used to be, but the thinned-out crowd actually contributes to the calm, relaxed atmosphere that the lighting, the decor, and the ambient music were designed to create all along. The people working at the counter are consistently friendly and it's an ideal place to head for when you're seeking a mellow vibe. Open: daily 10-24. (Map area C6)

De Rokerij - Lange Leidsedwarsstraat 41, 622-9442

www.rokerij.net

Who would guess that in the middle of this touristy strip there's a great coffeeshop? The decor in here is a mixture of Asian motifs. The music is spacey, but not sleepy, and there are lots of comfortable nooks to settle into. It's a popular spot and you can tell that they have a lot of regulars hanging out. On weekends it's packed! My only complaints are that drinks are pricey and that they don't let you park your bike out front. Open: sun-thurs 10-1; fri/sat 'til 3. (Map area C7)

De Rokerij - Singel 8, 422-6643

This Rokerij is one of the nicest coffeeshops in the Central Station area. There are African-influenced murals on the walls, and low, cushioned seats. Just make sure that you don't sit under one of the spotlights that fade in and out from time to time: unless you're a bit of an exhibitionist, it can be very annoying to be catching a good buzz and suddenly find yourself on centre stage. They also serve alcohol. Check the little blackboard by the entrance to see which nights they're offering freebies like tarot reading or foot massage. (For the record there's another, smaller, Rokerij at Amstel 8.) Singel branch open: sun-thurs 9-1; fri/sat 'til 2. (Map area D3)

De Overkant Hortus - Nieuwe Herengracht 71

This shop is located right across the canal from the Botanical Gardens (see Museums chapter), close to the Waterlooplein market (see Shopping chapter). It's a small shop, but the simple, uncluttered interior and the big windows make it feel airy and open. The big mirror makes for an interesting effect when you walk into the bathroom. Smoking a joint here and then exploring the Gardens is a great way to spend an afternoon. Open: mon-sat 10-24; sun 12-24. (Map area F6)

Kashmir Lounge - Jan Pieter Heijestraat 85-87, 683-2268

This whole place is adorned with Indian metal-work lampshades, embroidered fabrics, and coloured-glass candle holders. One incense-laden room is furnished with patterned carpets, pillows decorated with mirrors, and low wooden tables. The quality of smoke is pretty good. DJs play from time to time and then the place gets pretty packed. In the afternoons it's very mellow. They have a small terrace out front in the summer, too. It's located not too far from the Ten Kate Market (see Shopping chapter). Open: mon-thurs 10-1; fri/sat 10-3; sun 11-1.

Homegrown Fantasy - Nieuwezijds Voorburgwal 87a, 627-5683

www.homegrownfantasy.org

For years, this well-known coffeeshop has had a good reputation for both the quality of their weed and the relaxed atmosphere of the shop. They stock a large, tasty selection of Dutch-grown grass and a couple of types of hash. They also serve pots of tea, as opposed to dinky little cups. I like it here best in the daytime when the light is soft and time just seems to slow... right...... down. Be sure to visit the toilet where the black light makes your teeth glow and your pee look like milk! Open: sun-thurs 9-24; fri/sat 'til 1. (Map area D4)

Siberië - Brouwersgracht 11, 623-5909

www.siberie.net

Siberië is a great coffeeshop that caters to an international crowd who appreciate the changing art exhibitions, cool tunes, and of course the smoke. They sell a good variety of dope in all price ranges. And they also have a computer where you can check your e-mail. Be sure to make time for a walk along the canal where they're located - it's very beautiful. Open: sun-thurs 11-23; fri/sat 11-24. (Map area D3)

de Republiek - 2de Nassaustraat 1a, 682-8431

www.republiek.net

This cute shop, with connections to Siberië (see above) and Ruigoord (see Festivals, Music chapter), is an institution in this neighbourhood. They've been around for ages, and locals are always dropping by for a smoke and a chat. It's not as busy as Siberië and therefore a little more restful. Upstairs you can check your e-mail. There's also a large assortment of teas including fresh mint and yogi. If you get the munchies, they sell fresh fruit by the piece. Open: daily 10-23. (Map area B2)

de Supermarkt - Frederik Hendrikstraat 69, 486-2497

www.desupermarkt.net

Another shop in the same family as Siberië and Republiek, the Supermarket has the same products available, and the same reasonable prices for drinks and snacks (they're one of the few places in town that didn't jack their prices with the introduction of the euro). Tea is €1.15; tostis or soup €1.60; Looza fruit juice €1.60. The big wood table at the front is a tranquil, warm spot to smoke and read a magazine when the afternoon sun spills in. It's off the beaten track, so you might want to combine a visit here with a meal at the Fridge (see Restaurants, Food chapter). Open: daily 11-23. (Map area A4)

Katsu - 1e Van Der Helststraat 70, 675-2617

www.katsu.nl

Katsu is a long-standing neighbourhood coffeeshop located just off the Albert Cuyp Market. It's got a shabby, homey feel to it, and some wicked grass. They're famous for their Hazes, which give a wonderful cerebral high. Their hash made with the Ice-O-Later (see Pollinator Co, Shopping chapter) is out of this world. Drinks are reasonably priced, there's a vaporizer, the music is good, and they have a pinball machine. Well worth a visit. Open: mon-thurs 11-23; fri/sat 11-24; sun 12-23.

YoYo - 2e Jan v.d. Heijdenstraat 79, 664-7173

YoYo is a perfect place to spend a mellow afternoon reading or writing, while you slowly smoke a joint. The shop is spacious and airy, which is particularly nice if you don't smoke tobacco. In warm weather there are tables out front on a car-free street. Don't expect to find big frosty buds here, but all their weeds are organically grown and produce a satisfying, mellow high. As it's a bit out of the centre (near Albert Cuyp Market), their prices are low. Buds are sold in €5 and €10 bags. Food and drink are also cheap: cheese tosti - €1.35; tea - €1.15; cappuccino €1.35. Open: mon-sat 12-19; sun 16-19. (Map area E8)

La Tertulia - Prinsengracht 312

www.coffeeshopamsterdam.com

Plants, flowers and a little fountain give this coffeeshop a tropical feeling, but what I like best about this place is the outdoor terrace they set up in the summer. It's right at the edge of the canal and there are flowers on all the tables. It's easy to find this building: just look for the Van Gogh sunflowers painted all over it. Open: tues-sat 11-19. (Map area C5)

Paradox - 1e Bloemdwarsstraat 2, 623-5639

www.paradoxamsterdam.demon.nl

Not only can you buy and smoke cannabis here, but the Paradox serves up some delicious food! Their awesome fruit shakes are a bit expensive, but if you've got the dough they're a real treat. A banana/strawberry shake, big enough to share, costs €3.90, and a giant glass of fresh orange juice is €2.30. They also cook up fresh, home-made soup. Nice decor, and the neighbourhood is beautiful. Open: daily 10-20 (but the kitchen closes at 16). (Map area B4)

Dutch Flowers - Singel 387, 624-7624

www.dutch-flowers.nl

The beautiful canal on one side and an interesting, busy little street on the other make this a nice spot to take a break. There's a stack of magazines and comics, and good music on the stereo. It's located right in the centre of the city by Spui Circle. Their selection of weed and hash is also available in small amounts. And they serve beer. Open: sun-thurs 10-1; fri/sat 'til 2. (Map area C6)

Any Day - Korte Kolksteeg 5, 420-8698

The first time I walked into this tiny, welcoming coffeeshop, the guy behind the counter offered me a hit from a vaporizer (which they sell here) before I even had my coat off! Now that's friendly service. It's not far from Central Station and seems to cater to an international crowd. Across the street there's a brothel with girls in the windows. Oh yeah, and the coffee is terrible - stick to tea or juice. Open: daily 10-1. (Map area D3)

Kadinsky - Rosmarijnsteeg 9, 624-7023

www.channels.nl/kadinsky.html

A hip coffeeshop with an area upstairs that's perfect for kicking back and smoking that first joint of the day. The music varies from acid jazz to reggae to rock - it just depends on who's working. Delicious cookies are also available. Located on a tiny little street near Spui Circle. They also have a tiny shop at Langebrugsteeg 7. Open: daily 10-1. (Map area D5)

The Bluebird - Sint Antoniesbreestraat 71, 622-5232

www.coffeeshopbluebird.nl

The huge, old menu at the Bluebird was famous for it's variety and the creative way it was displayed. Current laws (see box) have forced them to cut back some on choice, but the quality of their wares remains high. The only problem with the Bluebird is that it's small and gets way too packed. If that's the case and you can't grab the comfy upstairs couch, you can always make a purchase and then wander down the street to the Museum Coffeeshop (see below). Open: daily 9:30-1. (Map area E5)

Museum Coffeeshop - Oude Doelenstraat 20, 623-5267

The owners of the Hash Marihuana Hemp Museum (just a few doors away) have done a nice job fixing up this place. There are lots of hemp decorations and some trippy murals. They don't sell smoke anymore, but you can bring in your own. The corner location and big windows make it a great spot for watching all the sleazy action on the street. Upstairs there's a beautiful, North African-style chill-space, but it's not always open so you should ask before you head up. Open: daily 10-1. (Map area E5)

Basjoe - Kloveniersburgwal 62, 627-3858

You can ask the owner for the exact pronunciation of his coffeeshop's name, but I'm pretty sure "Bashoo" is close. Anyway, it's a very pleasant shop, populated by travellers who've wandered in and made it their local while they're in town. The menu features some quality weed and hash, and the music is usually alright, too: the last time I was in they were playing *James Brown's Funky People*. If the weather's good, there are a few small tables out front by the canal. Open: sun-thurs 10-1; fri/sat 10-2. (Map area D5)

Greenhouse - Oudezijds Voorburgwal 191, 627-1739

www.greenhouse.org

Little lights embedded in the walls here gradually change colour, and the ceiling, tables and wash-room walls are encrusted with sea shells. Whether it's the decor or the good buds, the list of celebrities who've visited this popular shop just keeps on growing. Sometimes it gets too crowded in here, but mostly it's an agreeable place to while away some time, especially if you can snag a seat out front on a sunny summer day. Open: sun-thurs 9-1; fri/sat 9-3 (Map area D5)

The Otherside - Reguliersdwarsstraat 6, 421-1014

As it's located right in the heart of the gay ghetto, it's mostly men that come here, but women are also welcome. It's a friendly spot and it's easy to meet people. The main draw-back is the dance music played too loud. Open: daily 11-1. (Map area D6)

Tweedy - Vondelstraat 104, 618-0344

www.tweedy.nl

Tweedy sits at the edge of Vondelpark just across the street from the Vondel Church. I find it a pleasant place to get stoned. I especially like sitting at the back in one of the three train com-partments, complete with overhead luggage racks full of magazines and backgammon sets. They also have a pool table, and a good selection of candy bars. Open: daily 11-24. (Map area A7)

De Kuil - Oudebrugsteeg 27, 623-4848

A slightly older crowd hangs here because of the classic rock on the sound-system. This area around the Damrak is pretty sleazy, but the shop itself is clean, comfortable, and very tourist friendly. They have a good selection of smoke on offer and it's one of those places where it's always 4:20. They also serve alcohol, though they advise you not to mix the two. Open: sun-thurs 12-1; fri/sat 12-3. (Map area D4)

seeds/grow shops

There are numerous reputable places to buy seeds around town, but over the past few years a lot of fly-by-night companies have also appeared selling inferior products. The reputable compa-nies have spent years developing their strains in order to produce a stable, reliable seed. I've listed a few of them below. Remember that while it's legal to buy cannabis seeds in the Netherlands, it's illegal to import them into most other countries. You've been warned.

Sagarmatha Seeds and Psychedelic Gallery - Marnixstraat 255, 638-4334

www.highestseeds.com

This company's motto, "highest on earth", refers in part to their name. Sagarmatha is what they call Mount Everest in Nepal. The 100%-organically-produced seeds sold here aren't super cheap, but they're aimed at connoisseurs, who will appreciate the end result. They sell some very tasty strains including Bubbleberry, Yumbolt, and the particularly pleasurable Matanuska Tundra (a.k.a. Alaskan Thunderfuck). Check their web site for news, images of resin-coated plants, and some interesting links (see also Smart Shops & 'Shroom Vendors, Shopping chapter). Open: mon-sat 12-17. (Map area B4)

Sensi Seed Bank - Oudezijds Achterburgwal 150, 624-0386

www.sensiseeds.com

The people who brought you the Hash Marijuana Hemp Museum run this business, too. You'll find everything you need for growing on sale here, starting with seeds. Like Sagarmatha, the seed prices are a bit high, but they have proven genetic quality and that attracts a lot of professional growers. They're always big winners at the Cannabis Cup awards (see Festivals, Music chapter). They sell a fat, full-colour catalogue with photos of beautiful buds for €2.50. They also have a small shop near Central Station, at Nieuwendijk 26. Open: sun-wed 11-18; thurs-sat 11-21. (Map area E5)

Pollinator Company - Nieuwe Herengracht 25, 470-8889

www.pollinatorcompany.com

Hash exhibit

This inviting shop caters to almost all your pre- and post-harvest needs. They invented and sell the amazing Pollinator (for making hash), and the incredible Ice-o-lator. It's un-fucking-believable how good the hash is that's made from this simple device. The owner has also selected seeds from several top seed companies that she believes "are some of the world's best strains to use for making hashish". Cool. Inside the door on your right is a display of hash from around the world. They also sell books, hemp products, smoking accessories (including a very nice vaporizer), and - as the space is shared by the Botanic Herbalist - psychoactive plants (see Smart Shops & 'Shroom Vendors, Shopping chapter). Open: mon-sat 11-20. (Map area E6)

T.H.Seeds - Nieuwendijk 13, 421-1762

www.thseeds.com

Hemp Works (see Hemp Stores, below) sell their own, in-house line - T.H.Seeds. They've been in business since 1993, and are well respected amongst growers in the know. Strains available include the incredible S.A.G.E., Chocolate Chunk, and their newest variety, The Hog. Make your purchase during their 4:20 happy hour, mention *Get Lost!*, and get 10% off! That's also when you're most likely to find their resident seed expert, Adam, in the house. He knows a fuck of a lot about growing and is happy to share his knowledge. Open: daily 12-19. (Map area D3)

Emerald Triangle Seed Company - Prins Hendrikkade 87, 777-2767

Interestingly, one of Amsterdam's newer seed companies is also it's oldest, selling original Seed Bank stock. Over many years these strains have earned the admiration of growers the world over. Stop by the "Home of the Haze" and check it out. Open: sun-thurs 11-19; fri/sat 11 'til late (though you may have to knock loudly to get in as the owner tends to snooze for awhile in the afternoon). (Map area E4)

The Flying Dutchman - Oudezijds Achterburgwal 131, 428-4023
www.flyingdutchmen.com

This company sells their seeds from an easy-going shop, with the same name, which is located in the Red Light District, just across the canal from the Cannabis College (see box). Choose from their own line, or from one of the other companies' products that are also available here. And take some time to look over their impressive selection of glass pipes. Open: daily 11-19. (Map area E5)

Soma Seeds
www.somaseeds.nl

Over the years, I've had the pleasure of smoking several varieties grown from Soma's organically-bred seeds. Absolutely delicious. They're available online and around town at places like Seeds of Passion (see below).

Seeds of Passion - Utrechtsestraat 26, 625-1100
www.seedsofpassion.nl

The interesting thing about this seed outlet is that they sell strains developed in countries other than Holland. They've also got a good selection from local seed companies. Open: mon-sat 11-18. (Map area E7)

hemp stores

Hemp Works - Nieuwendijk 13, 421-1762
www.hempworks.nl

This hemp store sells designer clothing: "industrial organic wear". Most of the clothes they carry - jeans, dresses, lingerie and more - are on their own label, and include unique, classy touches like their sewn-in, patented rolling-paper dispensers. Or the secret stash pockets in their popular winter coat, The HoodLamb. They also sell a wide variety of fresh mushrooms, hand-blown glass pipes, and a choice selection of knick-knacks that make good presents for the discerning smoker back home. New this year are the cool hemp fashions from Kanabeach. You'll also find flyers for clubs and parties, and information about coffeeshops, all displayed against a backdrop of hemp walls and heavy sounds from the hip-hop and drum & bass DJs that spin at the back of the shop. Open: daily 12-19. (Map area D3)

Pollinator Company - Nieuwe Herengracht 25, 470-8889
www.pollinatorcompany.com

This shop really is unique. As if all the other great stuff available here wasn't enough (see Grow Shops, above), they're also well stocked with hemp products: clothing from Euro-American Marketing (*www.hemp-amsterdam.com*), food (try the delicious hemp-burger mix), oils, and lots more. Open: mon-sat 11-20. (Map area E6)

Sensi Seeds Hemp Store - Oudezijds Achterburgwal 148, 624-0386

The owners of the Hash Marihuana Hemp Museum have some exciting plans for a broad-range hemp store at this address, with unique products produced right here in the Netherlands as well as others from around the world. It's still in the planning stages, but hopefully it'll be open by the time you get here. (Map area E5)

A NOTE ON DRUGS IN AMSTERDAM

Once again Holland leads the western world in progressive thinking and action: soft drugs like cannabis and hashish have been decriminalized for over 25 years. Small amounts of these harmless substances can be bought, sold, and consumed without interference by the police.

Trafficking in hard drugs is dealt with seriously, but addiction is considered a matter of health and social well-being rather than a criminal or law enforcement problem. The number of addicts in Holland, where they can receive treatment without fear of criminal prosecution, is much lower than other countries where the law is used to strip people of their human rights (not to mention their property).

Some member states of the European Union (especially France), are putting pressure on Holland to conform to their repressive drug laws. This has resulted in the introduction of new drug policies that, while still more liberal than elsewhere, reflect a regressive trend in the thinking of the Dutch authorities.

The Cannabis College - Oudezijds. Achterburgwal 124, 423-4420

www.cannabiscollege.com

This non-profit organization was formed in order to educate the public about the cannabis plant and all it's uses. The volunteers who run the college are also dedicated to bringing about an end to the insane and unreasonable punishments inflicted throughout the world on those who choose to use cannabis, for whatever reason. They're located in a 17th-century canal house. Stop in to look at the exhibits and see what events are going on. If you want to visit their beautiful garden in the basement, they ask for a suggested donation of €2.50, which is used to help fund the college. Open: daily 11-19 (possibly longer in summer; shorter in winter). (Map area D5)

Shopping

Saturdays, at 17 or 18:00, most stores in Amsterdam lock their doors and they don't open again until Monday afternoon. However, many stores in "tourist areas" are now allowed to open on Sunday. Most stores stay open on Thursday nights until 21:00.

markets

Albert Cuypmarkt - Albert Cuypstraat (between Ferdinand Bolstraat & Van Woustraat)

www.albertcuypmarkt.com

It's big and it's great! Amsterdam's most famous market is crowded with stalls and shoppers. You'll find everything here, from fruits and veggies, to clothes and hardware. Underwear is a good deal and so are plain cotton t-shirts (if yours are getting smelly). Just remember that you don't pick your own fruit and some of the vendors are assholes and will routinely slip a few rotten pieces into each bag. This happens to tourists and Dutch shoppers alike, so don't take it personally and don't be afraid to complain. To pick your own produce, shop at the Turkish stores that are found around most markets. Open: mon-sat 9-16. (Map area E8)

Organic Farmers' Market - Noordermarkt

Its location at the foot of the Noorderkerk (North Church) lends a medieval feel to this fantastic organic market. All the booths sell healthy produce and products. Consequently, it's not really cheap, but if you like markets it's well worth a visit. Right around the corner, on the same day, is the Lindengracht market (see below). Another organic market (that also takes place on Saturdays) can be found at Nieuwmarkt (see Public Squares, Hanging Out chapter) from 9 to 16:00. The Organic Farmers' Market is open on Saturdays from 9 to 16:00, too. (Map area C3)

Lindenmarkt - Lindengracht

This is an all-purpose market that's a bit more expensive than Albert Cuyp, but still has some good deals. It's in a beautiful neighbourhood and is right around the corner from the Organic Farmers' Market (see above). An easy way to get to this and the Noordermarkt is with the *Opstapper* mini-bus from Central Station, Waterlooplein, or anywhere along the Prinsengracht (see Public Transport, Getting Around chapter). Open: sat 9-15. (Map area C3)

Noordermarkt - Noordermarkt

For all you die-hard shoppers with nowhere else to go on Monday morning, this market's for you. There's both used and new clothes, books, records, and all kinds of junk. Great for bargain hunting. After it closes you can often find good stuff in the garbage. And just for the record, there have been markets at this location since 1627! Open: mon 9-12. (Map area C3)

Dappermarkt - Dapperstraat

A lot of immigrants from North Africa and the Middle East shop at this all-purpose market, which is the cheapest in Amsterdam. There's also an Egyptian guy there who sells tasty falafels. It's close to Oosterpark (see Parks, Hanging Out chapter), the Tropenmuseum (see Museum chaper), and the windmill (see Ij Brewery, Bars chapter). Open: mon-sat 9-16. (Map area H7)

Ten Kate Market - Ten Katestraat

It's a bit out of the way for most tourists, but if you're in the area pay a visit to this lively neighbourhood market. Kinkerstraat, the main shopping street running by Ten Katestraat, lacks charm, but the streets and canals behind the market are pretty. It's near the Kashmir Lounge (see Coffeeshops, Cannabis chapter). Open: mon-sat 9-17. (Map area A6)

Waterlooplein Market - Waterlooplein

This square is home to a terrific flea market where you can find clothes and jewellery and all kinds of junk. It's easy to spend a couple of hours wandering around and, unlike other Amsterdam markets, you can try bargaining. Open: mon-sat 10-17. (Map area E6)

Flower Market - Singel

This pretty market is full of flowers and plants that are sold from barges on the Singel canal between Koningsplein and Muntplein. There are lots of good deals and it's probably the best place to buy tulip bulbs. Even if you're not interested in shopping here, it's a pretty market to wander through. (Map area D6)

books & magazines

The American Book Center - Kalverstraat 185, 625-5537

www.abc.nl

I think this is the cheapest store in Amsterdam for new books, especially for students, who get a 10% discount. They're located on the Kalverstraat, one of the main car-free shopping streets in the city. With five busy floors, ABC is the largest source of English-language books in Europe. Look for bargains in the basement. They also have a great selection of magazines. A few times a year they clear out all the back issues on the main floor, and you can sometimes find some good stuff for a euro or two. If you're here on the American Thanksgiving, everything in the store is discounted by 10%! The American Bookstore also hosts an interesting project called the ABC Treehouse (Voetboogstraat 11; *www.treehouse.abc.nl*). In a cosy gallery nearby, volunteers from the bookstore present author lectures, writers' workshops, and (on the last Friday of every month) a lively open mike night. Bookstore open: mon-sat 10-20 (thurs 'til 21); sun 11-18:30. (Map area D5)

Barry's Book Exchange - Kloveniersburgwal 58, 626-6266

Everything is very well organized in this clean shop (there's none of that mustiness associated with so many used book stores) and you're bound to find something of interest. They have a big travel section with both guides and literature, and there's a German and French section, too. If you have some books to sell, I find that they pay the fairest price in town. Open: mon-fri 10-18; sat 10-17:30; sun 11:30-16. (Map area E5)

Kok Antiquariaat - Oude Hoogstraat 14-18, 623-1191

www.nvva.nl/kok

This is one of the best used bookstores in Amsterdam. It's spacious and well organized, with a lot of English titles. English literature is upstairs. Open: mon-fri 9:30-18; sat 9:30-17. (Map area D5)

De Slegte - Kalverstraat 48-52, 622-5933

www.deslegte.nl

Some good deals on remainders can be found at this big store on the Kalverstraat. It lacks the charm of KOK (see above), but upstairs you'll find a huge selection of used books, many in English (I recently found a rare Philip K. Dick novel for €4). Open: mon 11-18; tues-fri 9:30-18 (thurs 'til 21); sat 9:30-18; sun 12-17. (Map area D5)

Evenaar - Singel 348, 624-6289

http://travel.to/evenaar

This travel bookshop has a fascinating collection. Works are organized by region and include not only guides and journals, but novels, political analyses and history - many by lesser known authors. Worth visiting for a browse if you're travelling onward from Holland. Open: mon-fri 12-18; sat 11-17. (Map area C5)

Athenaeum Nieuwscentrum - Spui 14-16, 624-2972

www.athenaeum.nl

For cheap magazines, check the bargain bin at this news shop on Spui Circle. I buy old *NME's* and other music mags here in the €.50 to €2 range. For new magazines and international papers, this is one of the best stores in Amsterdam. The sister bookstore next door is excellent, but not cheap. Open: mon-sat 8-21; sun 10-18. (Map area D5)

Vrolijk - Paleisstraat 135, 623-5142

www.vrolijk.nu

This shop advertises itself as "the largest gay and lesbian bookstore on the continent". It's located just off the Dam Square and it's usually pretty busy. If you're looking for something in particular, the staff are friendly and helpful. Open: mon 11-18; tues-fri 10-18 (thurs 'til 21); sat 10-17. (Map area D5)

Vrouwen in Druk - Westermarkt 5, 624-5003

A small, women's bookstore across from the beautiful, old Westerkerk and the Homomonument. Mostly used books as well as magazines and postcards. Open: mon-fri 11-18; sat 11-17. (Map area C4)

Intermale - Spuistraat 251, 625 0009

www.intermale.nl

This is a gay bookstore. It's a nice space with a good selection of books, magazines and some videos. They have gay guides to countries all around the world and a small porno section in the back. Open: mon 11-18; tues-sat 10-18; (thurs 'til 21). (Map area C5)

Book Traffic - Leliegracht 50, 620-4690

The owner of this used bookshop's got lots of English books and, sometimes, a bargain bin out front. There are a few other used bookshops located on this beautiful canal, too. Open: mon-fri 10-18; sat 11-18; sun 13-18. (Map area C4)

Het Fort Van Sjakoo - Jodenbreestraat 24, 625-8979

www.xs4all.nl/~sjakoo

"Specializes in Libertarian and radical ideas from the first to the fifth world and beyond". In addition to political books from around the world, this volunteer-run shop has a whole wall of fanzines and magazines, including lots of info on anarchism and squatting. They've got music, cards, stickers, and shirts, too. Definitely worth a visit. Open: mon-fri 11-18; sat 11-17. (Map area E6)

Would you buy an anarchist book from this man?

Muzikat - St. Antoniesbreestraat 3G, 320-0386

You'll find this unique little shop hidden away on an ugly stretch of road near the Nieuwmarkt. Muzikat specializes in music books. The shelves are full of biographies, lyrics, photo books, and histories of bands and genres. There are also some magazines and posters, and a couple of crates of vinyl. You never know, you might just find that Serge Gainsbourg tome you've been looking for. A few doors down at number 15 is a cool little record store called Gigantic. Muzikat open: tues-sat 12-18. (Map area E5)

Henk Lee's Comics & Manga Store - Zeedijk 136, 421-3688

www.comics.nl

Located in Amsterdam's tiny Chinatown, Henk's store is stuffed full of comics, toys, and trading cards. His specialty is manga, so check here if you're into that. Other shops to check for manga are Profesor Ich (Koninginneweg 218; 675-5663), or the bookshop in the basement of the Japanese-owned Hotel Okura (Ferdinand Bolstraat 333; 679-9238). Henk Lee open: mon-sat 11-18 (thurs 'til 21); sun 12-18. (Map area E4)

Gallerie Lambiek - Kerkstraat 78, 626-7543

www.lambiek.net

This is the most famous comic store in Amsterdam. They've got new, used and fanzines too. There's also a big selection of posters, and they host regular exhibitions. It's interesting to look over all the European comics. Open: mon-fri 11-18; sat 11-17; sun 13-17. (Map area C7)

Vandal Com-x - Rozengracht 31, 420-2144

www.vandalcomx.com

Definitely check this place out if you're into action figures: they've got them from floor to ceiling. It's where I got my much-admired "Radioactive Cornholio". They also sell trading cards, shirts, and more. The comix are at their other shop a few doors down the street. Open: tues-fri 11-18; sat 11-17; sun 12-17. (Map area B5)

Cultural - Gashuismolensteeg 4

This hole-in-the wall bookstore has a few shelves of English paperbacks and a few piles of *Life* and other magazines from the '50s and '60s (I scored a Johnny Cash cover and a Mohammed Ali). It's not far from Dam square in a pretty area, so you might pass it while wandering about, but I forgot to check the opening hours. Sorry. (Map area C5)

Oudemanhuis Boekenmarkt - Oudemanhuispoort

This little book market is located in the neighbourhood of the university, in a covered alleyway that runs between Oudezijds Achterburgwal and Kloveniersburgwal. Used books and maga-zines in several languages are spread out on tables and stands. There are also maps, cards and, occasionally, funny pornographic etchings from centuries past for a couple of euros. In the middle there's an entrance to a pretty courtyard with benches where you can rest your legs. Open: mon-sat 10-16. (Map area E5)

records & CDs

Boudisque - Haringpakkerssteeg 10-18, 623-2603

www.boudisque.nl

This is one of Amsterdam's best music stores. They have a big selection and they know what's hot. Lots of pop, punk, metal and dance, as well as music from all around the world. Mostly CDs, but still some vinyl. Pop into their excellent video and DVD shop next door, too. Open: mon 12-18; tues-sat 10-18 (thurs 'til 21); sun 12-18. (Map area E3)

Concerto - Utrechtsestraat 54-60, 624-5467

www.concerto.nu

New and used records, tapes and CDs in a pretty neighbourhood. It's a big shop with good prices on used stuff and lots of vinyl. Well worth checking out. Open: mon-sat 10-18 (thurs 'til 21); sun 12-18. (Map area E7)

Get Records - Utrechtsestraat 105, 622-3441

www.getrecords.nl

While they mostly carry CDs here, there's still some vinyl that's worth digging into. It's a great shop with a very select, up-to-date collection of pop, indie, funk, etc. Occasionally, they have live performances in the store. Open: mon 12-18; tues-sat 10-18 (thurs 'til 21); sun 12-18. (Map area E7)

Fat Beats - Singel 10, 423-0886

www.fatbeats.com

Fat Beats is the store to check out if you're looking for the newest hip-hop on vinyl. Much of it is independent and underground - there's a lot of white label stuff here. You'll also find some r&b and funk. DJs often hang out and spin a few tracks in the basement. Also for sale is a small selection of CDs, magazines, and clothing. Open: mon-sat 12-19 (thurs 'til 21); sun 12-18. (Map area D3)

Staalplaat - Staalkade 6, 625-4176

www.staalplaat.com

You'll find this store appropriately located in a stark, concrete basement not far from the Waterlooplein flea market (see Markets, this chapter). It stocks a huge selection of under-ground music: industrial, experimental, electronic, noise. They fill mail orders world-wide. This is also a good place to look for flyers advertising live performances of experimental music. Open: mon-fri 11-18; sat 12-17. (Map area E6)

Wentelwereld - 1e Bloemdwarsstraat 13a, 622-2330

I was riding through the Jordaan neighbourhood and my eye spotted the row of €1.25 bins at this used record store. I came out with a copy of *The Runaways Live in Japan*. They also sell comics, books, and DVDs. Open: tues-sat 12-17:30. (Map area B4)

Back Beat Records - Egelantiersstraat 19, 627-1657

www.backbeat.nl

Jazz, soul, funk, pop, blues, r&b: there's a lot of vinyl and CDs packed into this store's three levels. It's not cheap, but what a selection. Like Wentelwereld, it's also located in the Jordaan. Open: mon-fri 11-18; sat 10-17. (Map area C4)

Record Palace - Weteringschans 33, 622-3904

www.record-palace.com

This is another good place for collectors: they have sections for most kinds of music. Check out their collection of autographed record covers on the wall. It's located across the street from the famous Paradiso (see Music chapter). Open: mon-fri 11-18; sat 11-17; sun 12-17. (Map area C7)

Distortion Records - Westerstraat 72, 627-0004

www.distortion.nl

They advertise "loads of noise, lo-fi, punk rock, and indie". But you'll also find jazz, soul, latin, and more. Collectors, especially of vinyl, are going to love this place. The owners here are definitely on top of things, and they have a good selection of dance music, too. They're located just up the street from the Noordermarkt (see Markets, this chapter). Open: tues-fri 11-18 (thurs 'til 21); sat 10-18. (Map area C3)

Record Mania - Ferdinand Bolstraat 30, 620-9912

www.recordmania.nl

Although they do carry some CDs, vinyl rules at this pretty shop in the Pijp district. It's wonderful to walk in and find yourself surrounded by full racks of LPs and singles just waiting to be browsed through. They also have some bargain bins starting at €.30. Open: mon-sat 12-18. (Map area C8)

Second Life Music - Prinsengracht 366, 06-454-26344

www.secondlifemusic.nl

Amsterdam's newest used record shop mainly sells vinyl, though they do have a few CDs. There are also used books for sale on the upper level. Open: tues-sun 13-18. (Map area B6)

Roots - Jonge Roelensteeg 6, 620-4470

www.rootsmusic.nl

Reggae lovers take note: the hole-in-the-wall in the alley that houses this shop is full of Jamaican beats - from roots to dancehall and beyond. Check the African section, too. They stock some vinyl, but most of their collection consists of CDs, including re-issues at affordable prices. The owners are a great source of information about festivals in and around Amsterdam. Open: tues-sat 10:30-18 (thurs 'til 21); sun 12:30-18. (Map area D5)

Subterranean Music - Spiegelgracht 6

Space is at a premium in this cosy basement shop, so the owners are very selective about what new and used CDs (no vinyl) they stock. And it shows: there are always choice items for sale. They're located in an old house just a stone's throw from the Rijksmuseum. Open: tues-sat 11-16 (thurs 'til 21). (Map area C7)

De Plaatboef - Rozengracht 40, 422-8777

www.plaatboef.nl

"The Record Thief" has several stores around Holland. The Amsterdam store is very popular. They sell new and used CDs and LPs. My friend snagged a really hot Fela Kuti record here for cheap. There's also a small box in the back which occasionally has old issues of *Mojo* and other music magazines for €1 to €2.50. Open: mon 12-18; tues-sat 10-18 (thurs 'til 21). (Map area B4)

Groove Connection - St. Nicolaasstraat 41, 624-7234

www.grooveconnection.nl

Apparently, this is a really popular place with DJs, who come to hear what's new and hot. I like it because it makes me feel stoned when I step inside. If you're into cool dance music, you should drop by. (You might also want to check Dance Tracks, Soul Food, and Killa Cutz, which are all close by on the Nieuwe Nieuwstraat.) Open: mon 14-18; tues-sat 11-18 (thurs 'til 21); sun 14-18. (Map area D4)

Sound of the Fifties - Prinsengracht 669, 623-9745

Funk, soul, jazz, r&b, gospel and more. Prices aren't super cheap, but there are some gems to be found here. New and used. Open: mon 13-18; tues-sat 11:30-18. (Map area C6)

Datzzit - Prinsengracht 306, 622-1195

This record store is full of collectables. And not just records. They also have books, posters, some old toys, and other stuff. Open: mon-sat 10-18; sun 12-18. (Map area C5)

Forever Changes - Bilderdijkstraat 148, 612-6378

This is a well-stocked store full of new and used records and CDs. They have really interesting stuff in many areas: '60s, punk, blues... and check out the singles boxes on the counter. There are also some fanzines. Open: mon 13-18; tues-fri 11-18:30; sat 11-18. (Map area A6)

Independent Outlet - Vijzelstraat 77, 421-2096

www.outlet.nl

Punk and hardcore central. Vinyl (of course), and CDs. An excellent store (see Misc. this chapter). Open: mon 1-18; tues-sat 11-18 (thurs 'til 21) (Map area D7)

used clothing stores

In Amsterdam, like everywhere else, the moment that the term "vintage" took off, the price of second-hand clothing skyrocketed. Nevertheless, here are a few shops where you might still find some good deals.

Episode - Waterlooplein 1, 320-3000

This nice-sized store is located at a corner of the Waterlooplein flea market (see Markets, Shopping chapter). They've got a good selection of clothes and accessories, a lot of it from the seventies. It gets picked over pretty fast, but because they're so busy, new stuff is being unpacked all the time. There's lots of used clothing throughout the market, too. Open: mon-sat 9:30-18. (Map area E6)

Zipper - Nieuwe Hoogstraat 10, 627-0353

It's worth visiting this split-level shop because, even though it's not super cheap, the owners know what style-conscious shoppers are looking for and stock accordingly. They also have another store at Huidenstraat 7. Open: mon-sat 11-18 (thurs 'til 21); sun 13-17. (Map area D5)

Wini - Haarlemmerstraat 29 - 427-9393

Wini is a popular shop just a few minutes walk from Central Station. It's packed full of retro fashions, including plenty of seasonal accessories (in case you didn't pack right for the weather). Again, it ain't cheap, but they do have some nice stuff. Open: mon 11-18; tues-sat 10-18 (thurs 'til 20). (Map Area D3)

club fashions

Amsterdam's club fashion shops stock a wide variety of designer labels, both international and local. They're also all good places to find flyers for parties.

ClubWearHouse - Spuistraat 242, 622-8766

www.clubwearhouse.com

Come inside and listen to young DJs (who are encouraged to come by and show off their stuff) while you check out wild clothing by new designers on their in-house label, CWH. The owners have been on top of the club scene for years and they've got a reputation for having tickets and flyers for all the best parties. Open: sun/mon 13-18, tues-sat 11-18:30 (thurs 'til 21). (Map area C5)

Cyberdog - Spuistraat 250

www.cyberdog.net

Conveniently located right next door to CWH is the futuristic home of one of the most extreme clothing labels for clubwear, Cyberdog. As well as the club stuff there's a kinky fetish line, and they've also expanded into urban fashions. Open: mon-sat 11-18 (thurs 'til 21). (Map area C5)

Diablo - Oudezijds Voorburgwal 242, 623-4506

www.diabolo-shop.nl

Lots of intriguing clothing and accessories await you in this dark, grungy store. Their collection, which is "strong in gothic, fetish and punk fashion" changes regularly. You should be able to find something new and different here, and at pretty reasonable prices. Open: mon-fri 11-18; sat 10-18. (Map area D5)

body art

Tattoo Peter - Nieuwebrugsteeg 28, 626-6372

www.tattoopeter.nl

Tattoo Peter is one of the oldest tattoo parlours in the world, so it's fitting that it's located in an alley at the edge of the Red Light District - one of the oldest areas of the city. You can feel the history in this classic shop. Check out their website too: there are some great old pics. Open: daily 12-20. (Map area E4)

House of Tattoos - Haarlemmerdijk 130c, 330-9046

www.houseoftattoos.nl

Sjap, the guy who opened this studio, used to work at Tattoo Peter (see above). He does custom work in a relaxed shop with a good vibe. There's also a very talented artist there named Claudia. They're usually pretty busy so try to arrange an appointment if you can. Open: mon-sat 11-18. (Map area C2)

Body Manipulations - Oude Hoogstraat 31, 420-8085

www.bodym-europe.com

A long time ago, they used to offer scarification and branding here, but now it's just piercing. The people who run the studio are more than happy to talk to you about the procedure and what pain (if any), is involved. They also have an excellent collection of books and magazines on the subject. Prices start at €5 for an ear piercing (not including stud), and €16 for cartilage. Lip or eyebrow starts at €27.50. And tongue, nipple, navel, clit, penis, etc, also start at €50 (excluding jewellery). Open: mon-fri 11-18 (thurs 'til 20). (Map area E5)

Cut the Crap Hairstudio - Haarlemmerplein 9, 638-4588

www.cutthecrap.nl

Cut the Crap is situated in a comfortably run-down old house west of Central Station. It's a very casual place where you can relax with a drink or a smoke, and listen to some tunes while you wait for your turn under the scissors. The stylists are talented, and the prices aren't too bad. Open: tues-sat 11-19. (Map area C2)

Housewives and Haircuts on Fire - Spuistraat 102, 422-1067

It's expensive, but if you're heading to the clubs and want to do something more funky to your head, then you might want to pay a visit to the hairdressers here. They specialize in colours, braids, dreads, etc. It's right in the centre of town. Open: mon-sat 11-19 (thurs 'til 22). (Map area D4)

chocolate

Bon Bon Jeanette - Available at Natuurwinkels (see Health Food, Food chapter)

So fucking good! Jeanette's amazing chocolates are all made with organic ingredients. And they contain one-third less sugar than most other chocolates.

Australian Homemade - Leidsestraat 101, 622-0897; Singel 437, 428-7533
www.australianhomemade.com

This company uses only natural ingredients (no preservatives, dyes, or artificial colouring) to produce ice-cream, milkshakes, and delicious chocolates. I usually pick-up a pre-packaged "bar", that contains 6 assorted chocolates, for €3.75. They're decorated with gold-leaf and are almost too pretty to eat. Open: sun/mon 12-18; tues-sat 10:30-18 (thurs 'til 21). (Map area C6)

Puccini Bomboni - Staalstraat 17, 626-5474

Created before your very eyes in this glamourous boutique, Puccini's luxurious bonbons have been known to induce moaning and swooning of the most pleasurable variety. Open: mon 12-18; tues-sat 9-18 (Map area D6)

Leonidas Bon Bons - Damstraat 15, 625-3497; Schiphol Airport 653-5077
www.leonidas.com

The Belgians know what they're doing when it comes to chocolate, even when they're a big company like this one. Their small (250 gram, €5) box of assorted chocolates makes a nice gift, and the price at the airport branch is the same as in the city. Grab some for yourself, too, and you won't have to eat that crappy airplane food! Damstraat branch open: mon-sat 9-18 (thurs 'til 21); sun 11-18. Schiphol open: daily 7-22. (Map area D5)

smart shops & 'shroom vendors

Some years ago, the Dutch Ministry of Health came to the conclusion that hallucinogenic mushrooms are not hazardous when they're used responsibly. For a while, dried and fresh mushrooms were sold openly, in specialized shops, all around the country. But now - perhaps due to the bad influence of that Shrub in the White House - they've been declared illegal. So far, however, it seems like the government has decided to continue to tolerate the sale of some of these little buggers. This means that you can still buy fresh (though not dried) magic mushrooms at reputable shops, where you should be correctly informed about the proper dosage, best consumption method, and effect you can expect. (Any changes to the situation will, of course, be posted on the *Get Lost!* website.)

Obviously, if mushrooms and spores are illegal where you're from (and they probably are) then I'm not recommending that you buy them for export.

'Shrooms are often sold at "smart shops". These shops specialize in legal, mostly herbal, mind- and mood-enhancers of various sorts: stimulants, aphrodisiacs, relaxants, and hallucinogens. Smart shops have sprung up all around town over the last few years. Here are a few of the more established and consistently reliable ones.

Kokopelli - Warmoesstraat 12, 421-7000

www.consciousdreams.nl/shops/amsterdam/kokopelli

Opened by the Conscious Dreams crew (see below), this is one of the hippest smart shops in Amsterdam. The space is beautiful - with a very mellow area at the back where you can drink a tea, surf the net, listen to DJs, and enjoy the beautiful view over the water. The staff are tourist-friendly, so feel free to ask for info on herbal ecstasy, mushrooms, smart drugs, or any of the other products on offer. There's talk of turning the basement into a living-room-like chill space for meditation and Ayahuasca sessions. It's located very close to Central Station. Open: daily 11-22. (Map area E4)

Conscious Dreams Dreamlounge - Kerkstraat 93, 626-6907

www.consciousdreams.nl

This was the first smart shop in the world! They pioneered the concept and it's always worth dropping into this shop/internet gallery to see what's new. They stock a good selection of smart drugs and they're happy to advise and inform you about their different uses. You can check e-mail (€1.20 for 15 minutes) or do some gaming at one of several high-speed computer terminals. You'll also find lots of flyers for parties. It's a very trippy place. Come in... and be experienced. Open: daily 11-19; closed Sundays in the winter. (Map area C7)

The Botanic Herbalist - Nieuwe Herengracht 58, 470-0889

www.pollinator.nl

A very cool store. This space, which they share with the Pollinator Company (see Grow Shops, Cannabis chapter), is a centre for people interested in psychoactive plants. Many are for sale, like the rare Salvia, and the staff at this laid-back shop know all about them and their uses. There are lots of hemp products for sale, too. Open: mon-sat 11-20. (Map area E6)

The Headshop - Kloveniersburgwal 39, 624-9061

www.headshop.nl

Fresh mushrooms are sold at competitive prices at this cool shop. It's conveniently located in the centre (see Misc. below). Open: mon-sat 11-18. (Map area E5)

Sagarmatha Seeds and Psychedelic Gallery - Marnixstraat 255, 638-4334

www.highestseeds.com

This shop, located in a cosy old storefront (see Seeds, Cannabis chapter), was the first in town to sell the fabled Philosophers' Stones. Yummy (the high, not the taste). Stop in for experienced advice. Open: mon-sat 12-17. (Map area B4)

Shayana Shop

www.shayanashop.com

This is the best online smart shop. Their site is well laid-out, easy to navigate, and very professional. I've ordered from them and my package arrived discretely only a couple of days later. They sell psychedelic herbs, legal joints, Ayahuasca kits, aphrodisiacs, cannabis seeds, books, and of course, mushrooms. Check their site to find out what products can be sent to your part of the world, and then enjoy. Open: always.

miscellaneous

The Headshop - Kloveniersburgwal 39, 624-9061

www.headshop.nl

Most, if not all, your drug paraphernalia needs can be met in the shops on the streets heading east off Dam square past the Grand Hotel Krasnapolsky (which, by the way, has very nice, clean toilets upstairs to the left off the lobby). I think the best store is The Headshop, which has been in business since 1968. Lots and lots of pipes, bongs and papers; plus books, magazines, postcards, stickers and the required collection of incense and Indian clothing. They also sell magic mushrooms. They have a good reputation and sometimes it gets very crowded. Open: mon-sat 11-18. (Map area E5)

Independent Outlet - Vijzelstraat 77, 421-2096

www.outlet.nl

IO is a way cool store selling punk and hardcore records, skateboards, shoes, hard-to-find fanzines and magazines, great lunch boxes, and more. Even the doors of the dressing rooms rock! The stylin' clothes on offer are pretty cheap for Northern Europe. This is also a good place to find out about skate events and where punk and hardcore bands are playing. And if you're lucky, you might be here when they have one of their in-store shows: ask at the counter. Open: mon 13-18; tues-sat 11-18 (thurs 'til 21). (Map area D7)

Open - Nieuwezijds Voorburgwal 291, 528-6963

www.openshopamsterdam.com

What a great idea: a funky gift shop with inexpensive stuff that's open when other shops are closed. The owner has an eye for fun, funny, and useful items that make unusual gifts. She sells cute clothing, make-up, toys, and bric-a-brac starting at €3. And the stock is always changing - look out for new CDs and videos, too. Open: daily 14-21 (or whenever the sign outside is lit up). (Map area C5)

Aboriginal Art and Instruments - Paleisstraat 137, 423-1333

www.aboriginalart.nl

This is the only store of it's kind in Europe, so it's no surprise that I'd never seen such beautiful didgeridoos until I wandered into this shop/gallery. The owner travels to the outback in Australia and hand-picks these unique instruments himself to make sure that he gets only the highest quality. Some of the world's most famous didgeridoo players have performed using instruments from this shop. Also for sale are CDs and other Aboriginal artwork. If you already have a didgeridoo, stop by for info about jam sessions and workshops. Open: tues-sat 12-18; sun 14-18. (Map area D5)

Shamanismo Botanica - Hemonystraat 51, 673-4682

The vibe is so relaxed and unassuming in this shop that I almost felt like I was visiting a friend's apartment. The interesting and varied items for sale here include an impressive selection of herbs and "ethno-botanical" plants from around the world, music and musical instruments, and new-agey stuff. If none of that interests you, plop down in the back and try one of the fresh, organic juices - they're cheap and delicious. On Thursday nights at 19:00 they serve up a healthy, vegan meal for only €7.50. It's best to call first and reserve, but be warned that it's a very hippie event and it's possible you could be subjected to music-making or group hugs with your after-dinner chai. Shop open: tues-sat 11:30-18.

The Fair Trade Shop - Heiligeweg 45, 625-2245

Crafts, clothes and jewellery from developing countries. Also: fair-trade coffee, tea, chocolate, nuts and wine. Lots of unusual gift ideas. It's not the cheapest store, but there are some deals, and the money is going back to the right people. Open: mon 13-18; tues-fri 10-18 (thurs 'til 21), sat 10-17:30; sun 12-17. (Map area D6)

African Ash - various locations

If you're a pot smoker then you already know that glass pipes are the way to go. The artisans at African Ash do beautiful work, whether they're making a simple pocket pipe, or an incredible dragon that wouldn't be out of place in a museum. You can buy their glass at several places around town including Hemp Works, the Flying Dutchman, and Kashmir Lounge (see Cannabis chapter).

Baba Souvenir Shop - Warmoesstraat 47, 428-2504

www.babashops.com

This is a clean, well-stocked shop full of drug paraphernalia, hemp accessories, books and more. Everything is nicely displayed, including a wide assortment of glass pipes. Open: daily 9-22:30. (Map area E4)

China Town Liquor Store - Geldersekade 94-96, 624-5229

For some reason I think that this liquor store is cheaper than others, but I don't really know if it's true. Anyway, this sleazy strip is where I buy my booze and a couple of doors down is a great Chinese supermarket, Wah Nam Hong. There's a swankier liquor store in the basement of the Albert Heijn on Nieuwezijds Voorburgwal, and in the Dirk van den Broek at the Heinekenplein (see Supermarkets, Food chapter) that's open longer hours. The China Town Liquor Store is open: mon-sat 9-18. (Map area E4)

Cash Converters - Amstelveenseweg 39, 685-0500

If you like collecting junk, swing by this second-hand store at the far end of Vondelpark. Some things are ridiculously overpriced, but other stuff is a steal. I bought a really nice turntable here for next to nothing. And I got a hot-air popcorn popper. My friend found a Funkadelic CD for €4. Anyway, don't go out of your way, but if you decide to sell your walkman or you're looking for something specific, it could be worth a visit. You can bargain here, too. Open: mon 13-18; tues-fri 10-18 (thurs 'til 21); sat 10-17.

Donalds E Jongelans - Noorderkerkstraat 18, 624-6888

You know when you walk into an old-style corner store and find a great pair of sunglasses in a dusty display case? That's what this store feels like, except it's not dusty. They have a fantastic selection of old (but not used) sunglasses and frames at reasonable prices. It's right behind the Noorderkerk, so you might want to stop in if you're at either of the markets held here (see Markets, this chapter). Open: mon-sat 11-18. (Map area C3)

De Witte Tandenwinkel - Runstraat 5, 623-3443

I love the window of this store. They have the world's largest collection of toothbrushes! All shapes, all sizes and styles. They make unusual gifts, and they don't weigh much - which is a bonus when you're travelling. Take a look if you're in the neighbourhood, which has become known as The 9 Streets. And if you want to splurge on something for someone special, check out the beautiful hand-made jewellery at Galerie Steimer, just two blocks away at Reestraat 25. I did. Open: mon 13-18; tues-fri 10-18; sat 10-17. (Map area C5)

Big Red Machine - Waterlooplein 75

www.brm-winkel.com

Here's a place where you can buy European biker mags, t-shirts, and this year's Hell's Angels Amsterdam calendar. Upstairs is an Angels bar. Oh yeah, and I would heed the warning in the window - "This shop belongs to the Hells Angels Amsterdam. Fuck with it and find out." Open: tues-sat 12-17. (Map area E5)

Studio Spui - Spui 4, 623-6926

Check this shop for good specials on film close to its expiry date. Open: mon 10:30-18; tues-fri 9:30-18 (thurs 'til 21); sat 10-17:30. (Map area D5)

Photo Processing - Kruidvat, Nieuwendijk 160, 423-0385

If you've got the time, this drug store is one of the cheapest place I know to get photos processed in Amsterdam. It takes two days and I had a roll of 24 colour prints, with doubles, done for €6.35. The Dirk van den Broek supermarket at Heinekenplein also develops film cheaply. One-hour processing is available at Hema photo (Kalverstraat 208; 626-8720) where 24 single prints cost about €11. That's a bit cheaper than the tourist places on the Damrak and Rokin. Photo booths, to have passport-sized photos taken (€3.50 for black and white / €4 for colour), can be found at Central Station. (Map area D8)

Kinko's Copy Center - Overtoom 62, 589-0910

I'm not crazy about this joint because every time I've had some work done here they haven't done a good job. But they're open 24 hours a day, 7 days a week, so if you need to send a fax you can do it after 20:00, when phone rates are cheaper. (Map area A7)

Postcards

If you don't care whether Amsterdam is pictured on the ones you send home, look for the Boomerang free postcard racks. You'll find them in movie theatre lobbies, cafés and bars all around town.

Hanging Out

This is the chapter for people who enjoy just wandering about the streets, seeing who's around, listening to music in the park, and for those of you who are really broke. During the warm months the streets and parks of Amsterdam come alive and you don't need a lot of money to find entertainment. I've also got a couple of suggestions for when it's rainy or cold.

parks

Amsterdam has many beautiful parks that are well used throughout the year, but particularly in the summer months when the sunset lingers for hours and the sky stays light 'til late. Picnics are very popular in Holland - you can invite all your friends at once, instead of just the small number that would otherwise fit in your apartment. After dark, however, it's best not to hang out in any of these parks alone.

Vondelpark

www.vondelpark.tv

When the weather is warm this is the most happening place in the city, especially on a Sunday. Crowds of people stroll through the park enjoying the sunshine and the circus-like atmosphere. Little paths lead through leafy woods and out into fields where people are throwing discs and kicking footbags. Old men fish in quiet ponds only minutes away from live music being performed in the band-shell. There's a gorgeous, fragrant rose garden and a meadow with cows, goats, and llamas. Brightly coloured parrots sit in the trees, and everywhere else, people lie half-dressed on the grass, reading, smoking joints, playing chess, and sleeping. Trams: 1, 2, 5, 6. (Map area A8)

Amsterdamse Bos (Woods)

www.amsterdamsebos.amsterdam.nl | www.amsterdamsebos.com

It's a bit of a trek to get out to this big patch of green, but what a gorgeous place. There are lots of winding bike and hiking paths, waterways, a gay cruising area, cafés, an open-air theatre, a Japanese garden complete with blooming cherry blossoms in the spring, and some wild parties when the weather is nice. In another part of the Bos is a big field where you can lie on your back and jets from nearby Schiphol airport fly really low right over you: not exactly peaceful, but I enjoy it! In the summer it's a great place to do mushrooms (see 'Shrooms, Shopping chapter). You can rent bikes here, and free maps and information are available from the Bosmuseum (on Koenenkade at the end of Bosbaan; 643-1414; open daily in the summer from 10 to 17:00). Buses: 170, 171, 172 from Central Station.

Oosterpark (East Park)

Lots of ducks and lots of toddlers waddle around this park that's full of people strolling along the water's edge and playing soccer in the big field. It also draws a lot of drummers (since that was banned in Vondelpark). The beautiful old band-shell is sometimes used for parties like the Oosterpark Festival in the first week of May, and the fantastic Roots Festival in June (*www.amsterdamroots.nl*). At the last couple of Holland Festivals (also in June; *www.hollandfestival.nl*) they set up huge screens in this park and broadcast live opera to crowds of picnickers. It's right by the Dappermarkt (see Markets, Shopping chapter), and the Tropenmuseum (see Museums chapter). Tram 9. (Map area G8)

Sarphatipark

This pretty little park is really close to the Albert Cuyp Market (see Markets, Shopping chapter), and Katsu and YoYo (see Coffeeshops, Cannabis chapter). If you get the fixings for a picnic you can go here to pig out and smoke. Trams: 24, 25.

Wertheimpark

This small park is located on a canal just a couple of blocks away from the Waterlooplein flea market (see Markets, Shopping chapter) and it's an ideal place to cool your heels and catch your breath after battling the market crowds. It's peaceful under the big trees by the water. It's also just around the corner from Bakker Wieteke (see Bread, Food chapter). Tram: 9. (Map area F6)

Amstelpark

One of the most wonderful features of this gorgeous park is the Rhododendron Valley. For a few weeks in the spring, the area is in full bloom, and on a sunny day the colours are breathtakingly intense. The whole park is bike-free, and it's full of winding walking paths that open onto tranquil clearings and gardens. Strangely, lots of chickens have made their home here. Amstelpark is south of the city centre, about a 20 to 30 minute bike ride along the Amstel river. Or you can get there by riding the sneltram (express tram) number 51 from Central Station to Rai Station and then walking for about 10 minutes.

public squares

Robin Nolan Trio

Leidseplein

If the weather is good there are sure to be street performers in this popular square who sometimes line up for their chance to entertain the throngs of tourists (and make some dough). A lot of these artists are very talented and you can see their professionalism as they work the crowds between each unicycling, fire-eating, juggling trick, and how they deal with the inevitable disruptive drunk. If you do have a good time watching these people be sure to drop something in the hat. At the far end of the square, in front of the big movie theatre, are some cool, bronze lizard sculptures. And just across the street from there, carved high up on the marble pillars, is that age-old proverb *"Homo Sapiens Non Urinat In Ventum"*, which is Latin for "don't piss in the wind". (Map area 7B)

Begijnhof

The Begijnhof is a famous old courtyard in the centre of Amsterdam. Look for an entrance behind the Amsterdam Historical Museum. There's also an entrance just off Spui Circle, through an arched doorway between Nieuwezijds Voorburgwal and the Esprit Café. Inside that entrance there's a plaque describing the interesting history of the residential buildings surrounding the pretty gardens inside. (Map area C6).

Museumplein

Some of Holland's most famous museums are situated around this giant square, hence the name. They've had all kinds of problems with the recent renovations, but except for the underground parking garages and the crummy skate ramps, it's pretty nice. The basketball courts are back if you want to shoot hoops. And sometimes in winter there's an ice-skating rink, with skate rental available. (Map area C8)

Dam Square

This huge, historic square in front of the palace has been completely renovated, and though it looks good, it's a mess to navigate. It's quiet in the winter, but there's almost always something going on in the summer. Unfortunately, a lot of pickpockets and other sleazy creeps like to hang around here. Keep your eyes open and don't buy drugs from any of the scummy dealers: you'll definitely get ripped off. (Map area D4)

Nieuwmarkt

You're pretty sure to come across the Nieuwmarkt during your wanderings through the city. It's located just at the edge of the Red Light District and it's hard to miss the beautiful castle-like building smack dab in the middle. It used to be a weigh station and now it's one of the many busy cafés in the area. The whole square is surrounded by small shops, bars and restaurants. The numerous outdoor terraces here are especially lively on sunny days, and are popular drinking spots at night. There's an organic market there on Saturdays (see Markets, Shopping chapter). And on New Year's Eve, thousands of people gather here to party and set off one of the most intense fire-works displays you'll ever witness. (Map area E5)

libraries

Public Library - main branch Prinsengracht 587, 523-0900

www.oba.nl

You have to be a member to borrow books, of course, but there's a lot to do here even if you're not. If you ask at the information desk inside they'll give you English newspapers and magazines to read. It's a good way to catch up on news if you've been travelling for awhile. They also have interesting photo exhibitions on the ground floor, and a row of computer terminals with free internet access. Computers can be reserved by phone or in person for a maximum of 30 minutes. Note that there are no facilities for downloading or printing. In the small cafeteria (see Cafés chapter), you'll find more newspapers and magazines from around the world, many in English. On the first floor there's a good selection of English fiction and any other section in the library will also have a lot of books and magazines in English. Comics are also on the first floor. The travel section on the third floor has shelves of books about Holland and any other country you might be heading to. On the fourth floor is a music section with lots of magazines, and a large CD collection with listening facilities. Finally, if you're looking for a flat or need to sell something, the bulletin board by the front entrance is well used. The collection at this library is still pretty good, but over the past few years the building has become increasingly crowded, dirty and under-staffed. And you have to pay to use the toilets too! Open: mon-13-21; tues-thurs 10-21; fri/sat 10-17; sun (oct-mar only) 13-17. (Map area C6)

Pintohuis Library - Sint Antoniesbreestraat 69, 624-3184

In the early '70s, the city had plans to demolish this 17th-century house in order to widen the street. Fortunately, it was saved by activists who squatted the building. After a complete restoration it was re-opened as a library. The little rooms, old wooden furniture and high ceilings covered with frescoes make it a wonderfully peaceful place to read or ponder for a while. Upstairs they host art exhibitions; the last one I saw was of erotic paintings. Not bad for a public library! Open: mon, wed 14-20; fri 14-17; sat 11-16. (Map area E5)

internet cafés

ASCII - 2e Kostverlorenkade 105-108

www.squat.net/ascii

This is totally cool: a volunteer-run internet café in an old squat, set up by "an international bunch of iconoclasts, geeks, tech terrorists, squatters, eco-warriors, and anarchists". All the low-tech computers, which run on the Linux operating system, have been donated or picked from the garbage. Internet access is free, and the café serves very cheap drinks and snacks (like organic bananas). The space is also used for workshops, experimental music performances, political meetings, and pirate radio broadcasts. Open: daily 14-19. (Map area E6)

easyEverything - Damrak 33; Reguliersbreestraat 22

www.easyeverything.com

5am in Amsterdam

Sex and drug sites are taboo at this corporate enterprise, but it's OK if you just want to check your e-mail. It's bright and busy - even in the middle of the night - and you can always find a terminal. Prices start at €.50, but you better have exact change because there aren't any humans working here. And the machines where you buy a ticket with a log-on ID, don't give change either. Drinks, brownies and other snacks are available (see All Night Eating, Food chapter). The Damrak location is right by Central Station. Open: daily 7:30-23:30. Reguliersbreestraat is by Rembrandtplein. Open: twenty-four seven.

The Mad Processor - Bloemgracht 82, 421-1482

www.madprocessor.com

This is the place to visit if you feel like doing some gaming. Their 25 computers, which include some Macs, are set up in two rooms. There's a nice view of the canal from the front room, and the back room, though larger, is cosy and sociable. Printers and scanners are also available. Gaming costs €1 for 15 minutes. Internet use costs €.50 for 10 minutes, but only €1 for a full hour on either of their two computers that run Linux. There's not so much available here in the way of food and beverages, but there's a candy vending machine to fuel your killing frenzies and they serve non-alcoholic drinks at the counter. Open: daily 14-24. (Map area D4)

snooker

De Keizers Snooker Club - Herengracht 256, 623-1586

There's nowhere I know to play free snooker in Amsterdam anymore, but you can play here for €5 an hour per table (up to 4 people) and that's a pretty good deal. This price is valid daily from 13 until 19:00. (Map area C5)

free concerts

Het Concertgebouw - Concertgebouwplein 2, 671-8345
www.concertgebouw.nl

Every Wednesday at 12:30 this famous concert hall, world-renowned for it's acoustics, throws open its doors to the proletariat for a free half-hour performance. These concerts are extremely popular so whether it's in the main hall (2000 seats) or the smaller one (500 seats), you should get there early. It's located at the far end of Museumplein. Closed in the summer.

Stopera Muziektheater - Waterlooplein 22, 625-5455
www.stopera.nl

Every Tuesday at 12:30 this modern concert hall, which is home to Amsterdam's ballet and opera, presents a free half-hour concert in its Boekman Zaal. It's also well-attended, so go early. Also closed in the summer months. (Map area E6)

Vondelpark Bandshell - Vondelpark
www.openluchttheater.nl

Free concerts are presented here in the summer (see Parks, this chapter). There's a stand with benches, but you can also often hear the music from the grass across the pond. You'll find a schedule posted at the main entrance to the park. (Map area A8)

Club Lek - Desmet Studios - Plantage Middenlaan 4a, 671-2222

I was sad when the movie theatre that was here closed down, but at least the space is still being used for cultural events - like the taping of the live radio show, Club Lek. Every Wednesday three bands play a short set in front of a studio audience. All types of music are played by both local and international artists. Often a band doing a show at the Melkweg or Paradiso will do a set here. Tickets are free, but you have to call to reserve (mon-wed 12-17). While you're there, check out the schedules of the other radio and TV shows that are taped on the premises. (Map area F6)

snowboarding & skateboarding

As much of it is several metres below sea level, Holland is probably one of the last places you'd think of for snowboarding. But Snow Planet (Heuvelweg 6, 0255-545-848; *www.snowplanet.nl*) has two hills that you can use for €15 an hour. Equipment rental is €5. It's out of town. To get there take bus 82 (towards Ijmuiden) from Sloterdijk metro station. Open: daily 9-23 (sept-apr); shorter hours in summer.

As for skateboarding, there's an excellent indoor bowl at the NDSM Werf (T.T. Neveritaweg; see Live Venues, Music chapter), but it's only open on Fridays from 19 to 22:00 so it gets pretty crowded. At the Villa Friekens squat (which like the NDSM is also in North Amsterdam - at Kadoelenweg 360), the Overground Skateboardpark has a street course that's open on Wednesdays from 17 to 21:00, Fridays 19 to 22:00, Saturdays 13 to 17:00, and Sundays 17 to 21:00. Admission is €3. There's also a small street course with some nice obstacles in Oosterpark (see Parks, above), and further east under the highway bridge by Flevopark there's a giant half-pipe. In the west, there's a pretty good mini-ramp and some other stuff at Frederik Hendrikplantsoen, but it's all metal and can get pretty slippery. West of there, on the Orteliuspad, there's a small cement park with a quarter-pipe, a small hip, a spine, and some street obstacles. At the square called Staringplein, you'll find three infamous inclines (with sketchy transitions) known as the Blue Banks. And, finally, if you don't mind going a bit out of the city there's a pretty cool outdoor skatepark in Hooftdorp. For more detailed advice and info, your best bet is to stop in at Independent Outlet (see Shopping chapter), or Subliminal (Nieuwendijk 134; 428-2606): they know what's up.

kite flying & juggling

Because it's flat and windy, Holland is a great country for kite flying, especially at the beach. They make some pretty cool, compact ones these days and a growing number of people are actually travelling with kites. Try Joe's Vliegerwinkel (Nieuwe Hoogstraat 19; 625-0139). They sell all kinds of kites, discs, and footbags, too. (Map area E5)

For any juggling props you need, from balls and clubs, to diabolos and torches, as well as info about juggling events around Holland and the rest of the world, stop by The Juggle Store (Staalstraat 3; 420-1980; *www.juggle-store.com*). They've also got an awesome selection of yoyos. Open: tues-sat 12(ish)-17. (Map area D6)

tower climbing & view gazing

Great views! Good exercise! *Get off your ass!*

Westerkerkstoren - Westermarkt.
The highest. Open: apr-sept; daily 10-17; €3. (Map area C4)

Zuiderkerkstoren - Zuiderkerk.
The oldest. Open: jun-sept; wed-sat 14-16 (on the hour); €2. (Map area E5)

Beurs van Berlage - Damrak 277.
The most expensive. Open: tues-sun 10-16; €5 (includes admission to their museum). (Map area D4)

Great views! No exercise! *Sit on your ass!*

Kalvertoren - Singel 457. Café on top of a shopping centre. Open: daily 10-18:30. (Map area D6).

Metz & Co. - Leidsestraat 34. Café on top of a department store. Open: mon 11-18; tues-sat 9:30-18 (thurs 'til 21); sun 12-17. (Map area C6)

NeMo - Oosterdok 2. I don't think this new science centre is worth the high admission price (see Museums), but if it's not too windy, the big public deck outside isn't a bad place to hang for a bit and look out over the city and the beautiful old boats in the surrounding docks. Just climb the big steps out front, and remember to take some munchies. In the summer they put out a bunch of bean bag chairs and and a bar, and charge a couple of euros to go up. Sometimes there are DJs, too. Open: sun-thurs 10-18 ('til 21:00 in July and August); fri/sat 10-21. (Map area F3)

sauna

Sauna Fenomeen - 1e Schinkelstraat 14, 671-6780

In spite of the fact that it's in a squat (now legalized), this health club is clean, modern, and well-equipped. People of all ages, shapes and sizes come here. When you enter, give your name and get a locker key from the reception booth on the right. On the left is a changing room with instructions and rules in both English and Dutch. You can bring your own towel or rent one here. Then get naked, have a shower, and try out the big sauna or the Turkish steam bath! There's also a café serving fresh fruit, sandwiches, juices and teas. It's a relaxing place to unwind and read the paper or just listen to music and veg. Also available at extra charges are massages, tranquillity tanks, and tanning beds. Monday is for women only, and the rest of the week is mixed. Thursday through Sunday are smoke-free. The price, if you're finished before 18:00, is €6. After that it's €8. It's located just past the western end of Vondelpark. Since it's a bit out of the centre, you might want to consider combining a visit here with dinner at MKZ (see Restaurants, Food chapter) or an event at OCCI (see Live Venues, Music chapter). Open: daily 13-23. Closed for two months in the summer.

cee-ment ponds

Zuiderbad - Hobbemastraat 26, 678-1390

90 years old. Beautifully restored. Naked swimming Sunday afternoon 16:30-17:30. And occasionally, live jazz while you swim! (Map area C8)

Mirandabad - De Mirandalaan 9, 646-2522

Indoor/outdoor. With whirlpool, wave machine, and tropical bath. South.

Flevoparkbad - Zeeburgerdijk 630, 692-5030

Heated outdoor pool. Open mid-may to early sept. East.

Bijlmerbad - Bijlmerpark 76, 697-2501

Disco swimming on Sunday afternoon. South-east.

Marnixbad - Marnixplein 9, 625-4843

In the centre. (Map area B3)

museums
Museums

There are so many museums in this city that it could take you weeks to see them all. I'm only going to tell you about some of the more unusual and lesser-known museums. For basic information about the big ones - like the Rijksmuseum and the Van Gogh Museum - check the end of this chapter. Almost all of them have websites that are jam-packed full of additional information.

the unusual ones

The Sex Museum - Damrak 18, 622-8376

www.sexmuseumamsterdam.nl

It's true that you could see just about everything that's on display here in the Red Light District for free, but admission is only €2.50 and it's fun to tell your friends you went to the Sex Museum. The exhibits, which were getting pretty run down over the years, have been fixed up and the museum is looking a lot better. I particularly like the pornography from the turn of the century. And the two 7-foot-high penis chairs that you can pose on. Don't forget your camera! Open: daily 10-23:30. (Map area E4)

The Erotic Museum - Oudezijds Achterburgwal 54, 624-7303

This collection is large (covering 5 floors) and varied, but unfortunately much of it is un-labelled. They have drawings by John Lennon, collages from Madonna's *Sex*, and a very ugly, very funny, pornotoon from Germany. You can also push a button that sets a dozen or so vibra-tors into action! There is a floor of hard-core videos and phone sex, and above that a rather tame S/M room. There's only one reference to gay male sex in the entire museum, however - a surprising omission considering Amsterdam's status as the gay capital of Europe. Admission: €5. Open: sun-thurs 11-1; sat/sun 11-2. (Map area E4)

The Hash Marihuana Hemp Museum - Oudezijds Achterburgwal 130, 623-5961

While this museum used to be simply a required stop on every smoker's list of places to visit, it's matured into an informative collection for anyone who's interested in alternative forms of energy, medicine or agriculture. The exhibit consists of photos, documents, videos and arti-facts dealing with all aspects of the amazing hemp plant: history, medicinal uses and cannabis culture. There's even a grow room. And if you're hungry for more info you can peruse their small reference library or pick up one of the free pamphlets on hemp and its uses that you'll find by the entrance. They also sell books, magazines, and hemp products (including seeds). Visitors who do smoke will be interested in meeting Eagle Bill, the guy who really popularized the Vaporizer. He's often there, demonstrating how it works. The vaporizer is a glass waterpipe that uses a powerful heat source to "vaporize" the THC-bearing resin without actually burning the weed in the bowl. It's a healthy alternative to filling your lungs with smoke, and it gets you wasted! He'll give you a free taste, but you should definitely make a small donation. Located in the Red Light District. Admission: €5.70. Open: daily 11-21. (Map area E5)

The Torture Museum - Singel 449, 320-6642

Don't leave Amsterdam without visiting this unique collection of torture instruments. It's very educational. You'll learn where expressions like "putting the pressure on" originated. The museum is nicely laid out in an old house and lit with dingy, dungeon lighting. Each object has a small plaque explaining its function, and by and on whom it was inflicted. Detailed drawings illustrate their use. If you aren't already aware of Christianity's bloody history this is the place to see, quite graphically, just what has been done to people in the name of "god". (And speaking of god, what do you get when you cross an agnostic, an insomniac, and a dyslexic? Someone who stays up all night wondering if there's a dog.) Admission: adults €5; students €4. Open: daily 10-23. (Map area E4)

Tropenmuseum - Linnaeusstraat 2, 568-8215

www.kit.nl/tropenmuseum

This is one of the big ones that's in every guidebook. I'm including it here because it's such an amazing place, yet many visitors choose to skip it. This beautiful old building in eastern Amsterdam houses a fantastic collection of artifacts and exhibits from and about the developing world. The permanent exhibition uses model villages, music, slide shows, and lots of push-button, hands-on displays to give you a feel for everyday life in these countries. There are also changing exhibitions in the central hall and in the photo gallery. At the entrance you'll find info on films and music being presented in the adjoining movie theatre (see Film chapter), though they're not included in the admission price. Admission: €6.80 (€3.40 if you're under 18). Open: daily 10-17. (Map area H7)

De Poezeboot (Cat Boat) - a houseboat on the Singel opposite #20, 625-8794

Attention cat lovers! This isn't really a museum, but what the fuck? Spend some time on this boat playing with dozens of love-hungry stray cats who now have a home thanks to donations from the public and the volunteers who help out here. The boat is free to visit, but you're expected to make a contribution on your way out. Grab a postcard for your cat back home. Open: daily 13-16. (Map area D3)

Electric Ladyland - The First Museum of Florescent Art - 2e Leliedwarsstraat 5, 420 3776

www.electric-lady-land.com

It took 7 years to complete this very tiny, very trippy museum in the basement of this small shop, and when you see it you'll know why. It includes an intricate cave-like environment where you can push buttons that light up different areas of the space and play Jimi Hendrix. There are also display cases where minerals and fluorescent artifacts from all over the world are displayed under lights of different wavelengths, revealing startling, hidden colours. A €5 donation gets you an informative booklet and access to the collection. Open: tues-sat 13-15. (Map area B4)

Woonboot Museum (Houseboat Museum) - across from Prinsengracht 296, 427-0750

www.houseboatmuseum.nl

The 89-year-old ship housing this museum will show you what it's like to live on one of Amsterdam's approximately 2500 houseboats. There are also scale models of other boats, photos, a slide show, and displays intended to answer all those questions you have about life on the canals. If you print the map on their website and bring it along, they'll give you a free poster of Amsterdam. Admission: €2.50. Open: wed-sun 11-17 (mar-oct); fri-sun 11-17 (nov-feb). (Map area C5)

Heineken Brewery - Stadhouderskade 78, 523-9436

www.heinekenexperience.com

I used to recommend this famous place, but the price has gone up to €7.50, it's no longer a working brewery, nor do they offer all-you-can-drink; so I'm not sure why you'd want to go there now. Open: tues-sun 10-18 (last tickets sold at 17). (Map area D8)

Condom Museum - Warmoesstraat 141, 627-4174

www.condomerie.com

This tiny museum is made up of a colourful assortment of condom packages from around the world. The display is housed in a small glass case in the Condomerie (see Sex Chapter). It doesn't take long to view the collection, but checking out the names and logos on the boxes (like the camouflage condom - "don't let them see you coming") is good for a laugh. Open: mon-sat 11-17. (Map area D4)

The Smallest House In Amsterdam - Singel 7

The front of this house is only 1.01 metres wide! Property taxes were based on the width of the front of the house when this one was built, so they were pretty clever. You can't go inside, but it's still cool to take a look if you're walking by. It's not a museum. People live there. I used to know somebody who lived in the third-smallest house in Amsterdam. She hated it when tourists would knock on her door to ask if they could look around the third-littlest house in Amsterdam, so don't do it. There are other tiny houses around, including: Haarlemmerstraat 43 (1.28 metres wide); Oude Hoogstraat 22 (2.02 metres wide); and Singel 166 (1.84 metres wide). (Map area D3)

Botanical Gardens (Hortus Botanicus) - Plantage Middenlaan 2A, 625-8411

www.dehortus.nl

Established in 1638, this is one of the oldest Botanical Gardens in the world. The collection includes thousands of species of plants and they're displayed in a wonderful variety of greenhouses and landscaped gardens. The largest building has both desert and rainforest environments, but my favourite is still the palm house - a beautiful old building. You'll find peyote in the cactus greenhouse and the butterfly room is also quite exciting. The café, the Orangerie, was just renovated and is very pleasant - airy, light, and full of plants and little birds hunting for crumbs lodged in the wicker chairs. Occasionally, classical music is performed live. Admission is €5, but if you're staying nearby you should consider an annual pass (€16 for one person or €30 for four); then you can drop in whenever and make full use of those comfy benches in the hothouses. Trams: 7, 9, 14. Open: mon-fri 9-17; sat/sun 11-17 (oct-apr 'til 16). (Map area F6)

De Burcht (National Trade Union Museum) - Henri Polaklaan 9, 624-1166

www.deburcht-vakbondsmuseum.nl

In the late 1800's, the famous architect Hendrik Berlage was commissioned to design the head office for the General Dutch Diamond Cutters Union. That union was the first in The Netherlands to win its workers the right to a vacation, and the first in the world to attain an eight-hour working day! The building is beautiful and it's fitting that it now houses this museum of the Dutch trade union movement. Most of the exhibits, which include displays about union activities of the past and present, are in Dutch, but a free English guide is available at the front desk. It kind of makes you want to get out your old, scratchy Woody Guthrie albums. Admission is €1.15 for card-carrying union members and €2.30 for the unorganized. Take tram 9 to Plantage Kerklaan. Open: tues-fri 11-17; sun 13-17. (Map area F6)

Museum Het Schip - Spaarndammerplantsoen 140, 418-2885

www.hetschip.nl

The Ship is the name of an awesome residential building designed by Michel de Klerk in the early 20th century. He worked within a famous architectural movement known as the Amsterdam School. The collection, located in a corner of the building that used to be a post office, consists of a short film; inter-active programs that are accessible on several computer terminals; and the amazing interior itself. Through these displays, you'll learn the fascinating history of the controversial Amsterdam School and the parallel rise of the social housing movement in Holland. It was radical stuff, comrades... and it still is. Bus 22 from Central Station. Admission: €2.50; students €1. Open: wed, thurs, sun 14-17.

FOAM - Keizersgracht 609, 551-6500

www.foam.nl

Amsterdam's new photography museum is located in an old canal house that's been tastefully renovated in a contemporary style. The space is open, airy, and welcoming. The exhibitions, which represent all aspects of the art, change frequently. My museum card and I are regular visitors. Admission is €3.50. Trams 16, 24, 25. Open: daily 10-17. (Map Area D6)

Open Monument Day - early September, throughout The Netherlands

www.openmonumentendag.nl | www.bmz.amsterdam.nl

On Open Monument Day over 3000 historical monuments in Holland - homes, windmills, courtyards, churches - that usually aren't accessible to the public, open their doors. On this day you can pop into any building that flies a flag with a key on it. For more info call 627-7706 or visit their site.

Eyeglass Museum (Brilmuseum) - Gasthuismolensteeg 7, 421-2414

www.brilmuseumamsterdam.nl

I thought this museum sounded kind of interesting - historical eyeglasses on display in an early 17th-century house. But my curiosity wasn't strong enough to warrant the €5 admission. Some of you 4-eyes might want to take a peek, though. Open: wed-fri 11:30-17:30; sat 11:30-17. (Map area C5)

Vrolik Museum - Meibergdreef 15, 566-4664

I haven't been here either, but listen to this: an 18th and 19th century collection of some professor and his son's embryological and anatomical specimens! Weird. It's out of the way in south-east Amsterdam. Open: Tuesday and Wednesday 14 'til 17:00, or by appointment. Have a good time; I'm off to watch *Frankenhooker* again.

the big ones

Here is some basic information on Amsterdam's biggest and most famous museums. They all have impressive collections and can get quite crowded during peak season. Once a year, in mid-April, there's a Museum Weekend - when all the big ones are free.

Under the Rijksmuseum

A Museum Card - good for one year - costs €35 (€15 if you're under 25!) and is available at most of these museums. It gets you in free or at a substantial discount to almost all the big ones in Holland. If you're planning to go to more than a few of these, are visiting other cities in The Netherlands, or are returning within a year, then it's a good deal. The size of the discount that the card entitles you to varies considerably from museum to museum and show to show, but the visit at which you purchase the card is always free; so if you're smart you'll check the current discount rates and buy your card at the museum where you'd otherwise have to pay the highest surcharge.

The Museum Nacht *(www.n8.nl)* is a very cool annual happening that's become enormously successful. For one night in early November, almost 40 of Amsterdam's museums open up after-hours and provide visitors with unconventional atmospheres in which to view the collections. In the past, the Stedelijk Museum has been transformed into a club lounge, there's been line dancing in the Rijksmuseum, and the Botanical Gardens offered a tour of the hallucinogenic plants in their collection. The €12 Museum Night pass includes entrance to the museums as well as transport by tram, bus and boat - a great deal.

Rijksmuseum - Stadhouderskade 42, 674-7000
www.rijksmuseum.nl
Home to 20 Rembrandts. Open: daily 10-17. €9; 18 and under, free. Trams: 2, 5. (Map area C8)

Vincent van Gogh Museum - Paulus Potterstraat 7, 570-5200
www.vangoghmuseum.nl
Open: daily 10-18. €7; 17 and under, €2.50. Trams: 2, 3, 5, 12. (Map area B8)

Anne Frank House - Prinsengracht 263, 556-7100
www.annefrank.nl
Open: daily 9-19 (apr-aug 31 'til 21). €6.50; 17 and under, €3. Trams: 13, 14, 17. (Map area C4)

Stedelijk Museum - Paulus Potterstraat 13, 573-2737
www.stedelijk.nl
Modern art. Open: daily 11-17. €5; 16 and under, €2.50. Trams: 2, 3, 5, 12, 16. (Map area B8)

Rembrandt House - Jodenbreestraat 4-6, 520-0400
www.rembrandthuis.nl
Open: mon-sat 10-17; sun 13-17. €7; 16 and under, €1.50. Trams: 9, 14. (Map area E6)

Amsterdam Historical Museum - Kalverstraat 92, 523-1822

www.ahm.nl

Open: mon-fri 10-17; sat/sun 11-17. €6; 16 and under, €3. Trams: 1, 2, 5, 11. (Map area D5)

Jewish Historical Museum - J. Daniël Meyerplein 2-4, 626-9945

www.jhm.nl

Open: daily 11-17. €5; 17 and under, €2.50. Trams: 9, 14. (Map area E6)

Portuguese Synagogue - Mr. Visserplein 3, 624-5351

Open: sun-thurs 10-16; fri 10-14. €4.50. Trams: 9, 14. (Map area E6)

WW2 Resistance Museum (Verzetsmuseum) - Plantage Kerklaan 61, 620-2535

www.verzetsmuseum.org

Open: mon 12-17; tues-fri 10-17; sat/sun 12-17. €4.50. Tram: 9. (Map area F6)

Willet-Holthuysen Museum - Herengracht 605, 523-1822

www.willetholthuysen.nl

17th-century canal house. Open: mon-fri 10-17; sat/sun 11-17. €4. Trams: 4, 9, 14. (Map area D6)

Hidden Church (Amstelkring) - Oudezijds Voorburgwal 40, 624-6604

www.museumamstelkring.nl

Open: mon-sat 10-17; sun 13-17. €6; students, €4. (Map area E4)

Maritime Museum (Scheepvaartmuseum) - Kattenburgerplein 1, 523-2222

www.scheepvaartmuseum.nl

Open: tues-sun 10-17; (in summer, mon 10-17). €7; 17 and under, €4. Buses: 22, 32. (Map area F5)

NeMo (Science Centre) - Oosterdok 2, 531-3233

www.e-nemo.nl

Open: tues-sun 10-17. €10. Bus 22. (Map area F5)

Kröller-Müller Museum - Hoge Veluwe National Park, 031-859-1041 / 031-859-1241

www.kmm.nl / www.hogeveluwe.nl

This museum is located in the middle of a huge park in the middle of Holland. It has a big, incredibly trippy sculpture garden and a fantastic collection of Van Gogh's. Free use of bikes on site. Should be experienced. The park is open during daylight hours; the museum: tues-sun 10-17. Admission to the park and museum is €10 (the park alone - €5); and parking costs €5.

Keukenhof - Lisse (southwest of Amsterdam) - 31-25-246-5555

www.keukenhof.nl

Every spring, flower-lovers from all around the world converge on this 32 hectare park to see Holland's finest bulbs in bloom. There are miles of winding forest paths and grand avenues, fountains of every shape and size, a Japanese garden, a maze, and many special pavilions for indoor plants. And over 6 million flowers, most of which are tulips. On a sunny day the colours and scents are breathtaking. Don't forget your camera. Getting there involves a train journey to Leiden, and then a bus ride which takes you through an area filled with commercial bulb fields. Admission is €11.50. Open: daily 8-19:30; end-mar 'til mid-may.

Many guidebooks say that Amsterdam doesn't have a "world class" music scene, unlike some of its neighbouring capital cities. What a load of shit, but that shouldn't come as a surprise with a yuppie term like "world class". In fact, even if you're only here for a couple of days you should be able to find all kinds of music. From community-run squats and old churches to dance halls and large clubs, this city is full of great venues and great musicians.

how to find out who's playing

A.U.B. - Leidseplein 26, 0900-0191 (€.40/min)

www.uitlijn.nl

The Amsterdams Uitburo (AUB) is the place to start a search into who's playing in town. You'll find listings of all the music happening in and around the city on display here as well as the schedules for the Paradiso, the Melkweg (see below), and the other bars and clubs that feature live music. There are also racks full of flyers and info about theatre and film. It's convenient to buy advance tickets here, in person or by phone, but there's an expensive service charge (about €2 per ticket). Buying them directly from the venues, or from record stores (see Shopping chapter), will usually save you a bit of money. Open: mon-sat 10-18 (thurs 'til 21); sun 12-18. (Map area C7)

Shark

www.underwateramsterdam.com

This popular English-language fanzine is a great source of info on what's happening at music spots around the city - alternative venues as well as mainstream. It appears monthly and can be picked up for free at cool shops, bars, and the AUB. It also features short articles, reviews, horoscopes, and queer info. Check out their web site for a searchable database of current events.

Way-Out: Alternative List

I don't know who publishes this one-page flyer, but I'm glad they do. It includes music listings for squat clubs and alternative movie theatres. It's also available at the AUB and in alternative venues around town.

Irie Reggae Web Site

www.irielion.com/irie

If you're into reggae, look up this comprehensive listing of reggae bands and sound systems playing around Holland.

live music/party venues

Paradiso - Weteringschans 6-8, 626-4521

www.paradiso.nl

I wanted to go to this concert hall since I was 14 and bought the album *Link Wray Live at the Paradiso*. Now I go all the time! Located in a beautiful old church, this is an awesome place to see live music. There's a big dance floor with balconies around it. Upstairs and in the basement, are smaller halls where different bands sometimes jam after the main event. This is also a great venue for parties and performance art. I've seen everything from balloons filled with joints dropping from the ceiling to a live sex performance piece. Musicians seem to love this place, and big name bands will often do gigs here if they're touring Europe. Tickets here and at the Melkweg (see below) usually go on sale 3 weeks before the show (though sometimes earlier for big names), and average in price from about €8 to €20. In addition, they charge a membership fee of €2.50, which buys you a card that's valid for one month. If you're going to a sold-out show it's a good idea to buy your membership in advance to avoid a long line-up at the door on the night of the show. Located just a stone's throw from Leidseplein. (Map area C7)

Melkweg (Milky Way) - Lijnbaansgracht 234, 531-8181

www.melkweg.nl

Amsterdam's other classic venue, the Melkweg, is located in a big warehouse (which used to be a dairy), on a canal just off Leidseplein. Prices are about the same as the Paradiso and they also charge a membership fee of €2.50. Most nights you'll find bands playing in the old hall, or in the bigger, "Max" (revoltingly named after its corporate sponsor, some crappy soft-drink). Also on the ground floor is a photo gallery, and the café/restaurant Eat@Jo's (admission to the gallery is free via the restaurant entrance at Marnixstraat 409 from Wednesday to Sunday, 13 to 20:00). Upstairs is a video room, a playhouse for live theatre (which is often in English), and a cinema (see Film chapter), which you can no longer explore before and after concerts: you have to pay a separate admission to each. Flyers listing Melkweg events are available by the front door of the club (even when it's closed). The box office is open from 19:30 on every night that there's a show and: mon-fri 13-17; sat/sun 16-18. (Map area C7)

OCCII (Onafhankelijk Cultureel Centrum In It) - Amstelveenseweg 134, 671-7778

www.occii.org

This cool squat club has been open for more than 17 years. There's always something going on here: live music of all types, cabarets, readings, and other happenings. Their small hall has a bar, a nice-sized stage, and a dance floor. It has a divey, comfortable atmosphere. Back by the entrance, an old stairway leads to the Kasbah café on the second floor. The music and crowds are diverse and fun. Admission is usually €3 to €6. Look for posters advertising their events or wander by. The complex also houses a sauna (see Sauna, Hanging Out chapter) and a restaurant (see MKZ, Food chapter). It's located at the far side of Vondelpark, across the street and to the left. They usually close for a while in the summer. Tram 2.

Academie (O.T. 3:01) - Overtoom 301, 779-4913

squat.net/overtoom301

Despite pressure to have the resident squatters evicted by those who would rather see this building rot than be used for non-profit purposes, volunteers have managed to create one of the most important cultural centres in the city on this site. The Academie (so named because it formerly housed a film academy) was sitting empty until a bunch of squatters moved in, fixed it up, and made it available to the public. Now new projects are being launched here all the time. There's a restaurant/bar (see De Peper, Food chapter), a movie theatre (see Film chapter), a darkroom, and studios which are used for dance, performance and workshops. There are also some great parties happening in both the restaurant and the big studios. DJs play regular gigs and musicians perform all styles of music. It's underground Amsterdam at its accessible best. Look for a copy of *Shark* or the *Way Out List* (see above) for their schedule. Tram 1. (Map area A7)

H******n Music Hall - Arena Boulevard 590, 409-7900

www.heinekenmusichall.nl

Since we have no real say in where our tax euros go, it was left to a corporation to fund the building of this new music hall. Enter Heineken. The idea is to bring bands to Amsterdam that draw more people than the clubs in the city can handle. Anyway, it's only a couple of years old, holds 5,500 people, and the acoustics are pretty damn good. It's worth looking into who's playing here while you're in town. It's located way out by the Amsterdam Arena stadium - from Central Station take Metro 54 (direction Gein) to Amsterdam Bijlmer and from there it's just a few minutes walk.

P***i Stage - Arena Boulevard 1, 0900-0194 (€.40 per minute)

www.pepsistage.nl

This building was a Broadway-style theatre for about five minutes before it went broke and was taken over by a shitty corporation and transformed into a music site. It's a plush venue - everything inside from the carpets to the chandeliers is brand-spanking new. Expect to find some pretty big names, both Dutch and international, playing here. It's right next to the Music Hall (see directly above).

Maloe Melo - Lijnbaansgracht 163, 420-4592

www.maloemelo.nl

They call this place the "home of the blues", but you're just as likely to catch a band playing punk, country, or rock. There's live music here every night and no cover charge. Walk to the back of the bar and you'll find the entrance to another room where the stage is. Don't be shy to push your way up to the front where there's a bit more space. This is a good spot to check out local talent. And if the band is bad, you can wander next door and see what's happening at the Korsakoff (see Bars chapter). The bar is open from 21:00 (music room from 22:30) until 3 on week nights, and 4 on the weekends. Trams: 6, 7, 10, 13, 14, 17. (Map area B5)

Winston - Warmoesstraat 123-129, 623-1380

www.winston.nl

There's all sorts of great stuff happening here at this old hotel and club: parties, poetry, art exhibitions, live music. It's a lively, fun spot. As well as regular long-running events like the popular trash-glam Club Vegas and The Big F, there are lounge nights, rap and hip-hop, disco parties, and more. Cover is usually €5. Located in the Red Light District. The entrance is just to the right of the hotel. Open: sun-thurs 20-3; fri/sat 20-4. (Map area D4)

Bimhuis - Oude Schans 73-77, 623-1361

www.bimhuis.nl

For more than 25 years this is where jazz lovers have been gathering. I find the actual hall a bit uncomfortable, though it is intimate, and the sound is excellent. Ticket prices average €10 to €18 and some hot musicians have played here. On Tuesdays they host jam sessions, and admission is free. In 2004 they're moving to a brand new building along the water east of Central Station. Other spots around town with free live jazz include Bourbon Street (Leidsekruisstraat 6; 623-3440), Alto Jazz (Korte Leidsedwarsstraat 115; 626-3249) and Casablanca (see below). Concerts at the Bimhuis start at 21:00 on Thursday through Saturday nights. (Map area E5)

Casablanca - Zeedijk 26, 625-5685

www.casablanca-amsterdam.nl

It's well past it's heyday as a famous jazz club, and a small beer will set you back €2.50, but there's no cover charge to hear live jazz here on Sunday through Thursday nights. On the weekends there's dancing and karaoke. Open: sun-wed 20-3; thurs-sat 20-4. (Map area E4)

Pompoen - Spuistraat 2, 521-3003

www.pompoen.nl

The Pompoen is a swank multi-media centre right in the middle of town. (A far cry from the crazy antics of the Drugs Peace House, which used to be housed in this building!) Six nights a week quality live jazz is performed in their intimate, yet spacious, restaurant/café. There's no cover charge if you're eating, but the food is expensive. Otherwise, the cover is around €5 so I usually just nurse a drink while I soak up the music. Live jazz is played every Tuesday to Saturday from 21:30. (Map area D3)

The Last Waterhole - Oudezijds Armsteeg 12, 624-4814

www.lastwaterhole.nl

Tucked away in a little alley in the Red Light District, this old bar has seen more than its share of live music over the years. It's a rock-and-blues-jam-session, Grateful-Dead-cover-band, some-where-to-catch-local-groups kind of place. Bands play every night (except Monday) at 22:00, and there's no cover charge. They have a very good sound system, but for some reason they recently removed all the couches and chairs and replaced them with really uncomfortable benches. And just in case you were wondering, the electric fans whirling away in the wash-rooms are to stop people from doing coke. Open: sun-thurs 11-2; fri/sat 11-4. (Map area B4)

AMP (Amsterdam Music Promotions) - KNSM Laan 13, 418-1111

www.ampstudios.nl

A lot of musicians hang out at the bar in this rehearsal space. There's live music a couple of nights a week: Wednesdays it's free to hear new bands, and Thursdays there's jazz (€7.50 includes one drink). On the weekends they also host parties - Goa trance, salsa, African. The rest of the week it's super mellow, and if you're around here checking out the famous new architecture of the area, it's a cool place to stop in and get a cup of tea or a beer, and maybe shoot a game of pool. Also in the neighbourhood, you'll find: End of the World (see Restaurants, Food chapter) and the Azart Ship (see Bars chapter). Open: sun-thurs 12-1; fri/sat 12-3. From Central Station take bus 32 (direction KNSM Eiland), or night bus 79 (ask the driver to let you off at Azartplein). (Map area I3)

Inrichting Alternative Dance Night - Various Locations

http://come.to/deinrichting

Goths, vampires and everyone else who likes to dress all in black when they go out dancing, have been gathering together at Inrichting events for years. The music ranges from industrial to neo-folk to noise, and the organizers go out of their way to create a genuinely gothic environment. However, with the eviction of so many squats over the last few years, they've been having trouble finding a suitable, stable venue. Check their website for news. To find other like-minded individuals around town, check out the Medusa parties *(www.medusa-amsterdam.nl)*, or stop by the goth café Legendz *(Kinkerstraat 45; 683-8513; www.legendz.nl)*.

King Shiloh Sound System - Various Locations

www.kingshiloh.nl

The organizers of this reggae sound system have been around for years and along with presenting dances on a regular basis, they also have a record label and a show on pirate Radio 100 (see Radio, below). They play regular gigs at OCCII (see above) and after most big reggae shows. Admission is usually about €5. Check the Irie Web Site (see above) for more info. Stay Positive.

Volta - Houtmankade 336, 682-6429

Lately, parties have been occurring every Friday night at this west-side cultural centre. The building's not too big, which makes for a nice, intimate atmosphere, while the high ceilings give some breathing space on a crowded night. Recently there've been DJs spinning hip-hop, ragga, jungle, and raï to a pretty young crowd. There's often live music of some sort on Thursday nights, and if you're travelling with an instrument, swing by for their free Wednesday night jam sessions. Admission to Volta is usually a very reasonable €3.50. (Map area B1)

Westergasfabriek - Haarlemmerweg 8-10, 581-0425

www.westergasfabriek.nl

This old factory complex consists of 15 industrial monuments and their surrounding grounds. The site hosts music and film festivals, parties, and performances. When its current renovations are completed it will continue to host all sorts of cultural events, as well as providing additional parkland for Amsterdam's west side. This is also the home of West Pacific (488-7778), a restaurant that hosts popular dance nights every weekend. (Map area A1)

Akhnaton - Nieuwezijds Kolk 25, 624-3396

www.akhnaton.nl

Well-known for their African and Latin American music nights, Akhnaton also features hip-hop parties, roots ragga nights and the occasional jazz/funk jam. African and salsa nights tend to draw a more smartly-dressed crowd than I'm used to, and it's a bit of a pick-up scene, but the music is really good. It's only a five minute walk from Central Station. Open most Friday and Saturday nights. Admission is usually about €7 to €10. (Map area D4)

Panama - Oostelijke Handelskade 4, 311-8686

www.panama.nl

The little organic fruit and vegetable market that used to be here got the boot so this club, theatre and restaurant could open. The beautiful old building it's in has been completely renovated and it looks great. There's dancing here several nights a week (latin, jazz, disco) with a steep entry of €12. Maybe this will turn into a hip place, but it's more likely to be a hangout for all the yuppies moving into this old harbour district. (Map area I4)

Theater de Cameleon - 3e Kostverlorenkade 35, 489-4656

www.decameleon.nl

Located at the far end of Vondelpark, Theater de Cameleon hosts non-commercial, alternative performances. They present plays, the occasional stand-up comic, and regular open-mike nights for music. At their monthly Club Cameleon evening, there's an open stage with comedy, street theatre, performance art, and anything else anyone wants to do. It's more of a Dutch scene, but there's still usually some English spoken, and it's always a laugh. Call ahead if you'd like to perform. Admission ranges from €2.50 on the open-stage night, up to €8.50 for other events. Closed in July and August.

ADM - Hornweg 6-8, 411-0081

www.contrast.org/adm

This huge building along the harbour west of Amsterdam was squatted a few years ago after sitting empty for 5 years. Their opening party featured performances by Bettie Serveert (who played a fantastic set of Velvet Underground covers), and The Ex. Every party I've been to here has been great. And because the owner of the building is an evil little fucker, the effort you make to get out here will be especially appreciated. If you're not up to the long bike ride, there's usually a shuttle bus that leaves from behind Central Station when they have a party. They also serve a three-course vegetarian meal in their café every Wednesday, Friday and Sunday from 18:00. The cost is €5. Call in the afternoon to reserve, and for directions.

NDSM Werf - T.T. Neveritaweg 15, Amsterdam North, 330-5480

www.ndsm.nl

After forcibly closing most of the affordable spaces for artists (and their audiences) in the centre, the City Council will help fund a complex on the site of an old wharf that's been squatted in North Amsterdam - far from any real estate that's currently of interest to their developer friends. Cynicism aside, it's pretty cool. There are already some good parties happening out here, and there are plans for cheap studios, performance spaces, a cinema, galleries, a skatepark (see Hanging Out chapter), and a café and restaurant. Although it's quite a trek to get out to this industrial area, the view over the water is gorgeous.

dance clubs

If you're into dance clubs, raves and parties, refer back to Club Fashions in the Shopping chapter: those stores all have party information. Clubs usually open at about 23:00 and close around 4 or 5:00. Most have a dress code.

Mazzo - Rozengracht 114, 626-7500

Relaxed and friendly. Open: wed-sun. (Map area B4)   **www.mazzo.nl**

Club More - Rozengracht 133, 528-7459

Trendy. Some women-only nights. Open: wed-sun. (Map area B4)   **www.expectmore.nl**

iT - Amstelstraat 24, 625-0111

Famous gay disco. Open: fri/sat. (Map area D6)   **www.it.nl**

De Trut - Bilderdijkstraat 156

Gay (mixed). In a legalized squat. Admission is only €1.50. Sunday nights only. Doors open at 23:00 and close at 23:30. (Map area A6)

Club 020 - Nieuwezijds Voorburgwal 163

New club near Dam Square. Open: wed-sun. (Map area D5)

Escape - Rembrandtplein 11, 622-1111

Popular, especially on Saturday. Open: thurs-sun. (Map area E6)   **www.escape.nl**

Sinners in Heaven - Wagenstraat 3-7, 620-1375

Trendy. Open: thurs-sat. (Map area E6)   **www.sinners.nl**

Back Door - Amstelstraat 32, 620-2333

Gay. Straight for Saturday night's Soul Kitchen. Open fri-sun. (Map area D6)   **www.backdoor.nl**

Dansen bij Jansen - Handboogstraat 11, 620-1779

Students. Open: daily. (Map area D6)   **www.dansenbijjansen.nl**

Odeon - Singel 460, 624-9711

More students. Open: thurs-sun. 3 floors. (Map area C6)   **www.odeontheater.nl**

Tonight - 's-Gravesandestraat 51, 694-7444

In the Hotel Arena (see Sleep chapter). (Map area G8)   **www.hotelarena.nl**

C.O.C. - Rozenstraat 14, 623-4079

Gay. Mixed dance on Fridays; women-only Saturday. (Map area C4)   **www.cocamsterdam.nl**

Club Waterl'eau - Stadhouderskade 25 - 679-1370

One-and-a-half-hour nightclub cruise. Departs every Friday and Saturday at midnight. €25.

radio

Radio 100 - 99.3FM

www.radio100.nl

This pirate radio station has been around since 1986, and it's the biggest independent radio station in Amsterdam. They broadcast a wide range of shows covering many subjects and all types of sounds. They play an outstanding selection of music from around the world. Their schedule is listed in *Shark* (see How to Find Out, this chapter) and they also broadcast online.

Radio de Vrije Keyser - 96.3FM

www.vrijekeyser.nl

Born out of the radical squat movement of the late-seventies, these old-timers on the pirate scene became famous for their diverse, sometimes crazy programming. They broadcast a mix of politics, squat news, and punk music every Tuesday from 12 to 20:00, and they're often on the scene, broadcasting live, from demonstrations and squat evictions around town. They also present a great TV show on the local station Salto A1 on Tuesday nights at 20:00.

Radio Patapoe - 97.3FM

http://freeteam.nl/patapoe

Power to the pirates. Except for a few brief down times, Patapoe has been broadcasting diverse programmes on the air since 1989. Most afternoons and evenings, they play all kinds of cool music. All with no commercials. Yes!

BBC World Service - 648AM

www.BBC.co.uk/worldservice

Okay, so it's not exactly alternative, but they have news in English every hour on the hour.

festivals

All year long there are festivals going on in and around Amsterdam. Most of the ones I've listed here are free. For any without precise dates, check with the tourist office.

Queen's Day - April 30, everywhere in Holland

The biggest and best party of the year happens in celebration of the Queen's birthday. (It's actually her mother's birthday, but Beatrix's is in January - a bad time for an outdoor party.) On this day, Amsterdam becomes one big, orange-coloured carnival of music and dancing and gallivanting and carousing. And the world's biggest flea market opens for business: almost anything can be bought or sold. Despite a slew of ridiculous new rules and regulations imposed by the City Council over the last couple of years, it's still unbelievably fun. Type "Queen's Day Amsterdam" into any search engine and you'll find hundreds of photos.

Bevrijdingsdag - May 5, Museumplein

This one celebrates Holland's liberation from the Nazis at the end of WW2: something worth celebrating. If you're interested in seeing some of the country's bigger bands, check this out. It's always a fun party. Fuck Nazis!

Positive Rave Organization Street Party
- late May / early June

www.positiverave.org

I never miss this annual street rave protesting the global war on drugs. The meeting place is usually at Dam Square or Museumplein. Then there's a lively dance through the town and out of the city centre (because the cops get nervous when the streets are liberated) to a place where all the sound-systems and their DJs can set up for the party. On the same day, street raves take place in cities all over the world.

Ruigoord Festival - June 21, Ruigoord

www.ruigoord.nl

Over twenty-five years ago this town just west of Amsterdam was squatted and turned into a very cool community of artists and free-thinkers. Now, due to a very sleazy harbour development project (which is just an excuse to bury toxic waste!), most of the beautiful nature around the town has been bulldozed and the inhabitants are being evicted. There were great parties at Ruigoord all year round, especially on full-moon nights, but their famous and very trippy summer solstice bash was always one of the best. There are still full-moon and other parties going on, and, at the church there (which was spared the wrecking ball), there are poetry readings and a regular Sunday afternoon open stage and cafe. For news and directions check their website.

Park Pop - late June, Zuiderpark, Den Haag

www.parkpop.nl

This has been Europe's biggest free pop festival for more than 20 years, and over three-hundred thousand people usually turn up. Every year sees an interesting line-up of performers playing all kinds of music, but you'll have to truck out to The Hague for this one. Check the website for details.

African Music Festival - first weekend in August, Delft

www.africanfestivaldelft.nl

Here's another festival that's outside of Amsterdam. This incredible feast of African music gets better every year. Some of Africa's best and most famous stars play here, in a football field outside of Delft. Tickets are about €14 if you buy them in advance. There's camping nearby or hop a train back to Amsterdam - they run all night. Check their website for the exact date.

Kwakoe Festival - mid-July to mid-August, Bijlmerpark, South-East Amsterdam

www.kwakoe.nl

With over half a million visitors, mostly of Surinamese, Antillean, and Ghanian origin, this is Holland's biggest multicultural festival. It takes place over 6 weekends every summer and admission is free. The biggest draw is the soccer games, but there's also lots of music, food and art. Visit their site or call 697-8821 for details.

Gay Pride Parade - first weekend in August

www.amsterdampride.nl

If you're here at the beginning of August make sure to see this fun, extravagant, and somewhat risqué procession of queer-filled boats cruising along the canals. Later in the day there are usually street parties and open air film screenings. Call the Gay & Lesbian Switchboard (see Phone Numbers chapter), or stop by Pink Point (see Practical Shit chapter) for information on the route.

Parade - mid-August, Martin Luther King Park

www.mobilearts.nl

This old-style European carnival is produced by the same trippy people who did the Boulevard of Broken Dreams some years ago. As the sun goes down on the circle of tents, barkers and performers compete to draw you inside, where you'll witness strange, otherworldly spectacles that defy the imagination. It's really something special. Admission is free until about 17:00 and then it's about €4. Once inside, most of the attractions also charge an admission fee, but it's fun just to hang out and people-watch, too.

Openhavenpodium (Open Harbour Stage)
- mid-August, Java Island

www.openhavenpodium.nl

This nautical festival takes place at one end of Java Island, which is east of Central Station. Over a weekend in August the area is transformed into a wonderful carnival with theatre, art exhibitions, films, and lots of activities on and in the water. During the day there are a lot of kids. At night, as the lights come on, it takes on a magical atmosphere similar to that of Parade (see above) with performances, lots of food and drink, dancing, and even lounges by the water. It costs about €4 to get in, then most events are free or pretty cheap. Bring your bike so you can explore the cool modern architecture in the area, too.

Uitmarkt - end of August, Museumplein & Leidseplein

www.uitmarkt.nl

To celebrate the beginning of the new cultural season, Amsterdam's streets overflow with theatre, dance, film, and live music. King Sunny Adé and Dick Dale have both played in recent years. Almost everything is free.

Seven Bridges Jazz Festival - early September, Reguliersgracht

www.sevenbridges.nl

Amsterdam's youngest jazz fest is a one day affair that brings together Dutch and international groups. It's a free event that takes place along a canal that's famous for it's picturesque seven bridges in a row.

Cannabis Cup Awards - third week of November

www.hightimes.com

High Times magazine hosts this marijuana harvest festival, and it's getting bigger every year. It's mainly an American affair with several days of cannabis-related events that culminate in the actual awards given for the best strains of grass and hash, and the best seed companies and coffeeshops. There are parties every night at the Melkweg, often with some hot bands playing. And there's a Hemp Expo which is definitely worth a visit.

New Year's Eve - December...uh...

If you're coming for New Year's Eve and want to be at an organized party, you should start checking the club and AUB websites at least a month in advance. All the popular venues sell out fast. Thousands of people also celebrate on the streets, especially at Nieuwmarkt (see Public Squares, Hanging Out chapter). It's wild.

Het Blauwe Theehuis (The Blue Teahouse) - Vondelpark, 662-0254

www.blauwetheehuis.nl

This circular, spaceship of a building is docked smack-dab in the middle of Vondelpark (see Hanging Out chapter). In the day, especially if it's sunny, the two outdoor terraces are packed with people soaking up the rays. They have several beers on tap, and from 9 to 16:00 they serve lots of soups, sandwiches and cakes in the €2 to €4 range. At night, the bar upstairs opens and it's a happening little spot with great atmosphere. There's often live jazz on Wednesdays. Saturday and Sunday is more of a party scene with DJs playing anything from rare grooves to motown to hip hop to afrobeat. And lately they've been showing 16mm films on Monday nights. Note that if you stay real late and the park is deserted when you leave it's best not wander about on your own - however tempting a moonlit stroll might be. Open: daily 9-24 (but if it's busy on the weekends, they sometimes stay open 'til 3). (Map area A8)

Vrankrijk - Spuistraat 216

www.vrankrijk.org

Even if this long-established squat bar didn't have a sign, you'd have no trouble finding it thanks to the building's wild paint job. Go late if you want to be in a crowd. Buzz to get inside. There you'll find a high-ceilinged room covered with political posters. Despite all the punks hanging around, they play all kinds of music. Occasionally, there are benefits with speakers, bands and videos to raise funds for an organization or a cause. Saturday nights there's dancing in the back room. Every Monday there's a queer night. The Vrankrijk is one of the cheapest bars in the city, and any profits are given away to worthy political and social causes. Open: mon-fri 22-2; fri/sat 'til 3. (Map area D5)

Café the Minds - Spuistraat 245, 623-6784

This is a comfortably run-down bar with a lot of character. It's located not far from the Vrankrijk. They have a pool table (only €.50!), a good pinball machine (5 balls), and they play grunge, rock and metal. It's a fun place to hang out and have a drink (beer is €1.25) while you decide where to go next. Open: daily 21-3. (Map area D5)

Tetra - Nieuwezijds Voorburgwal 89, 625-8804

Tetra was recently opened by the same people who own and operate Homegrown Fantasy, right next door (see Coffeeshops, Cannabis chapter). The bar doesn't sell weed, but it is, of course, extremely smoker friendly. It's a chill place, with couches by the window and DJs playing an eclectic mix every night. Drinks are reasonably priced for this part of town: beer is €1.50; tequila €2. Open: sun-thurs 16-01; fri/sat 16-03. (Map area D4)

Modern Dance Café Vaaghuizen - Nieuwe Nieuwstraat 17, 420-1751
www.vaaghuyzen.net

I've seen several bars come and go at this location, but this one has definitely got it together. They bill themselves as a "before clubbing hangout" and DJs play there every night from about 21:00 - jazz and rare grooves, techno, breakbeats, lounge. The split-level space offers a cosy chill-room upstairs and a bar with a little backroom lounge down below. It's a very cool little spot. Open: sun 14-1; mon-thurs 17-1; fri 17-3; sat 14-3. (Map area D4)

Weber - Marnixstraat 397, 622-9910

Before you leave this popular joint because it seems too crowded, take a peek downstairs where you'll find a basement room decked out with old couches, big armchairs, lots of candles and a little greenhouse. It's a great place to sit around and shoot the shit with some friends, even if the beer is a bit overpriced. Its location close to Leidseplein is a plus. Open: sun-thurs 20-3; fri/sat 'til 4. (Map area B7)

Lux - Marnixstraat 403, 422-1412

Just a few doors down from Weber, and done up in much the same style, is this funky place. DJs play here several nights a week, spinning stuff from pop to new wave to drum and bass. Open: sun-thurs 20-3; fri/sat 'til 4. (Map area B7)

De Koe (The Cow) - Marnixstraat 381, 625-4482
www.cafedekoe.nl

One block further along Marnixstraat you'll find The Cow, which is less trendy than Lux and Weber. It's a pleasant place to escape from the crowds of nearby Leidseplein and hear some blues or rock. In the front you'll find backgammon sets and other games. Downstairs, after 18:00, they serve meals that start at €7.95. Open: sun-thurs 16-1; fri/sat 16-3. (Map area B7)

Soundgarden - Marnixstraat 164-166, 620-2853

The giant photos of Iggy and Henry in here set the tone for music that's played loud and grungy, much to the appreciation of the leather-clad dudes and chicks that hang here. Actually, a lot of different kinds of people drop in for a night of pool, darts and pinball. Also, the terrace over the canal out back is a great spot to smoke a joint and have a drink in the summer. Open: sun 15-1; mon-fri 13-1; sat 15-3. (Map area B5)

De Hoogte - Nieuwe Hoogstraat 2a, 626-0604

For my dough, this is the best bar along this strip. It's one of the cheapest, too. The good music, relaxed atmosphere, and online computers in the back draw in a cool crowd of all ages. From the window there's a view of the incessant, frenzied bike and pedestrian traffic on the street. It's right next door to The Headshop (see Misc, Shopping chapter). Open: mon-thurs 10-1; fri/sat 10-3; sun 12-1. (Map area E5)

Brouwerij 't IJ - Funenkade 7, 622-8325
www.brouwerijhetij.nl

For those of you who are in town for only a short time, here's your chance to do two tourist essentials at once: drink a Dutch beer other than Heineken and see a windmill. The brewery, in an old bathhouse next to this beautiful old mill, sells its delicious draft (with alcohol content up to 9 percent!) to a grateful crowd of regulars in its smoky, noisy pub. On sunny days the terrace is packed, but it's nicer across the street along the canal. It's a bit out of the centre, not far from the Dappermarkt (see Markets, Shopping chapter) and the Tropenmuseum (see Museums chapter). Open: wed-sun 15-20. (Map area H6)

Korsakoff - Lijnbaansgracht 161, 625-7854

The Korsakoff has always been a fun place to dance to punk, grunge, industrial, and the odd tune by Prince, but since their recent extensive renovations it's been a bit unclear what direction they're going move in. Traditionally, it's a fairly young crowd that hangs here and whatever happens it'll probably remain a cool place. Buzz to get in. Open: sun-thurs 23-3; fri/sat 'til 4. (Map area B4)

Kingfisher - Ferdinand Bolstraat 24, 671-2395

Located in a district known as the Pijp (which is pronounced "pipe"), the Kingfisher is an ideal place to plop your ass down and rest a bit after exploring the neighbourhood. During the day, light streams in through the corner windows and it's a casual, comfortable place to linger over a light meal or a warm drink. In the evenings, it's a warm and mellow hangout. And at night, when the alcohol starts flowing, it becomes a lively local bar. Open: mon-thurs 11-01; fri/sat 11-03. (Map area C8)

Getto - Warmoesstraat 51, 421-5151
www.getto.nl

This queer hangout is very different from the famous leather bars that share this strip of the Red Light District. It's a restaurant and bar that's decked out in an arty, comfortable style and it draws a fashionable, mixed crowd. In fact, in stark contrast with all the other bars in the area, there are probably more women here than men. Occasionally there are special theme nights, and anytime there's bingo expect a full house. Getto is open: tues-thurs 16-1; fri/sat 16-2; sun 16-24. (Map area E4)

Lime - Zeedijk 104, 639-3020

Whether you're looking for a chill place to hang with a few friends, or just want to have an intimate conversation with someone, this is one of the nicest places to lounge for awhile, especially earlier in the evening before it gets too crowded. The well-designed interior and arty decor make the space feel bigger than it is, and fresh, like the name. Open: tues-sun from 17. (Map area E4)

De Buurvrouw - St Pieterpoortsteeg 29, 625-9654

www.debuurvrouw.nl

They've been booking lots of acoustic acts here lately (can't be too noisy cuz of the neighbours), and it's a cool spot to hang out, listen to some music and have a drink. They also host open stage nights for stand-up comedy, poetry and music. Saturdays feature DJs and it gets super busy. Open: daily 20-3. (Map area D5)

De Diepte - St Pieterpoortsteeg 3-5

Just down the way from De Buurvrouw, in the same tiny alley, look for the sign with the devil and you'll find De Diepte. It's a late-night bar that gets packed in the early hours. Sometimes live bands play there, but mostly it's just a noisy crowd enjoying the music ("beat, garage, punk & roll-o-rama") and beer. (Map area D5)

De Duivel (The Devil) - Reguliersdwarsstraat 87, 626-6184

www.deduivel.nl

Years ago, this was the first bar in Amsterdam to play hip-hop on a regular basis. Now their DJs are expanding a bit and throwing in a little funk here, some breakbeats there. Weekends can get really busy. Weeknights are mellower. Peace to all the tourists, cuz I got a lotta love. Open: sun-thurs 20-3; fri/sat 'til 4. (Map area D6)

De Pits - Bosboom Toussaintstraat 60, 612-0362

www.cafedepits.nl

You'd think this bar was any ordinary Dutch drinking spot, what with its wood floor, pinball machine, pool table and dartboards. But instead of traditional Dutch sing-alongs, they play punk, hardcore and ska. The owners are friendly and will play requests. You should stop by if you want to know who's playing this sort of music around Amsterdam: there are usually flyers on the bar and sometimes they host gigs there, too. Open: tues-thurs 15-1; fri/sat 15-3; sun 15-1. (Map area A6)

Suite - Sint Nicolaasstraat 43

The only trace left of the fish restaurant that used to occupy this space, is the open kitchen where they now prepare quality hors d'oeuvres. They're delicious, but the tab runs up quickly if you make a meal of it. It's couches, candles and easy chairs make it an ideal spot to lounge with some friends. The DJs dish up mellow sounds. It's fashionable and chill. Open: mon 18-12; tues-sun 18-1 (fri/sat 'til 3). (Map area D4)

Vakzuid - Olympische Stadion 35, 570-8400

www.vakzuid.nl

The 1928 Olympics were held in Amsterdam and the stadium built for the occasion was recently renovated. The south side houses this restaurant/bar. The food's too expensive for me - actually, so are the drinks - but I love the lounge downstairs. With it's low, comfortable couches and fake fireplaces, it looks like a 1970's suburban den. And the view of the track and field is awesome. There are DJs on weekends, but for truly relaxed lounging I recommend weekday afternoons when the place is almost empty. In the summer there's a cushy terrace out front - ideal for recovering from the long bike ride out here. Open: mon-thurs 10-1; fri 10-3; sat 12-3; sun 12-1.

Café Saarein 2 - Elandsstraat 119, 623-4901

www.saarein.com

This famous, old-school dyke bar used to be one of the few women-only spaces in town. A few years ago it was sold and renovated, and while it remains a gay café, it now caters to a trendier, mixed clientele. The neighbourhood and the building are both pretty and interesting, and it's a pleasant place to stop in for a meal, or a beer and a game of pool or pinball. Open: sun-thurs 17-1; fri/sat 17-2. (Map area B5)

Azart (Ship of Fools) - KNSM Eiland

www.azart.org

I wrote about the bar on this old ship in the very first edition of *Get Lost!*, before the artists on board sailed away for a tour around the world that lasted years. Now they're back (at least temporarily), and docked in the same old spot on KNSM Eiland (behind the AMP - see Music chapter). When they're here, they have a bar that opens on Fridays nights around 10, and at 11:00 there's live music, skits, poetry, and anything else the residents dream up during the week. It's a little grungy - the toilet's only for women and guys are expected to pee into the water off the edge of a plank (it feels great!) - but the atmosphere is fun and very welcoming. It's a bit of a trek out here, so you might want to combine it with dinner at End of the World (see Restaurants, Food chapter). Ride your bike or, from Central Station, take bus 32 or 59 (direction KNSM Eiland) or night bus 79 (ask the driver to let you off at Azartplein). (Map area J3)

De Bierkoning (The Beer King) - Paleisstraat 125, 625-2336

www.bierkoning.nl

It's not a bar, but if you're into beer you'll love this shop which is located just a stone's throw from Dam Square. Wall to wall, ceiling to floor, beer awaits you in bottles of every shape and size. It's all neatly arranged by country, with an entire wall devoted to Belgian brews. You can grab a cold one to go, or if you're flying home from Amsterdam, some of the more exotic beers make great presents. Check out the special offers - free beer mugs with certain purchases, and 10 free beer coasters with every purchase (hey, free is free). The only beer I didn't see here was Duff. Open: mon-13-19; tues-fri 11-19 (thurs 'til 21); sat 11-18; sun 13-17. (Map area D5)

The great thing about being a visitor to Amsterdam and seeing a movie is that the Dutch never dub films. They're always shown in their original language, with Dutch subtitles. The 15 minute "*pauze*" in the middle of movies, an unwelcome intermission that always came at the worst moment, has thankfully been phased out at all but a couple of theatres. Most now boast about their no *pauze* policy, but if it matters to you and you don't see any notices about it, you can always ask before you buy your ticket.

Prices range from €5.80 to €8.75, with evenings, weekends, and holidays being the most expensive times. Some longer movies may cost even more, so always ask the price. The City, de Munt, and the Tuschinski sometimes offer weekend morning screenings for €4 or €4.50.

In keeping with the global trend, big chains are driving most of the independent theatres in Holland out of business, but the few that are still managing to hang on are included in the list below.

For movie listings pick up the *Film Agenda*, a free weekly summary of what's playing. It's published every Thursday and is available in bars and theatres. Each of the big commercial cinemas also posts a schedule of all the current first-run screenings in Amsterdam near their main entrance. The AUB (see Music chapter) has the schedules of most of the independents, and *Shark* (see Music again) also lists alternative film events. Online, you can find out what's playing at: *www.filmladder.nl* (click on Amsterdam).

theatres

Tuschinski - Reguliersbreestraat 26-28, 626-2633

This incredible Art Deco theatre opened in 1921, and just underwent a complete renovation that's restored it to its original splendour. It might just be the most beautiful movie theatre anywhere. The prices are a bit higher than some of the other cinemas in town, but it's worth it to watch a film from the comfort of the plush seats in the main hall (theatre #1). Occasionally - usually on Sunday mornings - classic silent films are screened with live organ music: quite an impressive spectacle. Go early so you'll have time to take in all the details of the decor in the ornate lobby and café (not to mention the bathrooms). (Map area D6)

Nederlands Film Museum - Vondelpark 3, 589-1400
www.filmmuseum.nl/index_eng.html

This museum/cinema/café is situated in a big old mansion in Vondelpark (see Hanging Out chapter). They screen a couple of different films every day in their two pretty little theatres. The admission price is €6.25 (€7.50 for longer films). You can pick up a monthly listing in the lobby. It's in Dutch, but check where the film was made because they show many from the US (VS) and Britain (GB). Also, some of the foreign films will have a little "eo" listed next to them, which stands for *engels ondertiteld* - English subtitles. They feature everything from old b+w classics, to rock 'n roll films, to women-in-prison flicks. Every Saturday night in the summer, weather permitting, a big screen is set up outside and a movie is shown for €2.50 (which includes a drink). The café is also very pleasant (see Vertigo, Cafés chapter). (Map area A8)

Film Museum Cinerama - Marnixstraat 400

www.filmmuseum.nl/cinerama

The film museum also screens first-run foreign and art films at this theatre near Leidseplein. If you see a film at the Calypso, which has two auditoriums in the same building, make sure you go to the bigger hall - the little one smells like old sweat. (Map area B7)

Filmhuis Cavia - Van Hallstraat 52-1, 681-1419

www.filmhuiscavia.nl

This little cinema lies just west of the city centre over a boxing club. It seats only about 40 and has an excellent rep program. They sell cheap beer in their café and admission is a very reasonable €4. Most films start at 20:30. Closed in summer. (Map area A2)

Kriterion - Roeterstraat 170, 623-1708

www.kriterion.nl

There's always an interesting mix of first-run and classic films being shown on the two screens of this student-run, art-house cinema. Especially popular is the Sneak Preview - a surprise screening of a new film every Tuesday at 22:00 (€4.50). Every so often they also present Club Cinema, with DJs and VJs playing into the night. The café in the lobby is busy and relaxed, and you can bring your glass of beer right into the theatre. Note though, that they sometimes stop the film for a *pauze*. Admission: sun-thurs €6.20; fri/sat €6.60. (Map area F7)

Cinema de Balie - Kleine-Gartmanplantsoen 10, 553-5100

www.balie.nl/cinema

The Balie is a true multimedia centre: film house, café, theatre, digital city, and gallery. They show very cool films (it was the only place in town that played *Battle Royale*), and many are in English. They have two theatres, and although the screen isn't very large in the smaller hall, the seats are much more comfortable. De Balie is located just off Leidseplein. Stop in to pick up their schedule (which is in Dutch and English). Admission is €6.25. (Map area C7)

Melkweg Cinema - Lijnbaansgracht 234-A, 531-8181

www.melkweg.nl

Upstairs at the Melkweg (see Live Venues, Music chapter), there's a small cinema that shows interesting retrospectives (films by Cronenberg, classic porn, or martial arts, for instance). Admission is €6. On Friday afternoons at 17:00 youngsters under 25 years of age can attend their special Moviezone feature for only €3.50. Otherwise, films cost €6 and usually start at 20:00. On weekends there's sometimes a second screening just after midnight. (Map area C7)

Cinecenter - Lijnbaansgracht 236, 623-6615

www.cinecenter.nl

On Sundays mornings at 11:00 the two small theatres here screen new features for only €5. The rest of the week they charge €6.50 for matinees, and €7.50 on evenings, weekends, and holidays. There's still an intermission slipped into some movies. The program consists mostly of foreign films, so make sure to confirm that the subtitles are in English. The Cinecenter is located right across the street from the Melkweg (see above). (Map area C7)

de Uitkijk - Prinsengracht 452, 623-7460

www.uitkijk.nl

When it opened in 1929, de Uitkijk was only the fourth art-house cinema in all of Europe. They still show arty first-run stuff here that most of the big theatres ignore. Located right by Leidsestraat and next door to Gary's Muffins (see Cafés chapter). Admission: matinees €6; all other screenings €7. (Map area C7)

Rialto - Ceintuurbaan 338, 676-8700

www.rialtofilm.nl

The Rialto is an independent that's partly run by volunteers. They show some interesting films in their two theatres, but they're mostly foreign, so remember to check the language of the subtitles before you enter. Admission is €5.50 on Monday; €6.50 Tuesday to Thursday; and €7.50 on the weekend. Along with the Melkweg (see above), the Rialto also co-hosts Moviezone *(www.moviezone.nl)*. If you're 25 or under, you can attend these weekly screenings for just €3.50. The films start at 15:30 on Friday and they show some pretty good stuff. "Grown-ups" pay full price.

Het Ketelhuis - Haarlemmerweg 8-10, 684-0090

www.ketelhuis.nl

This is the first and only cinema dedicated exclusively to Dutch film. As long as it's Dutch they'll screen it - popular, obscure, short, animated... even films made for TV. It's quite unique. The theatre is located on the grounds of the Westergasfabriek (see Music chapter). If this sounds interesting to you, it's worth giving them a call as some of the programs have English subtitles. Price: €6.80. (Map area A1)

Smart Cinema - 1e Constantijn Huygenstraat 20, 427-5951

www.smartprojectspace.net

Located in the hulk of a building that houses the Smart Project Space (see Cafés chapter), this small, comfortable theatre shows experimental films and videos as well as "alternative" Hollywood films (Coen Brothers, Lynch, etc). It's convenient that you can hang out in the restaurant/café before and after the film, but unfortunately the sounds from the DJ across the hall occasionally seep into the theatre: it can be distracting, to say the least. There are plans to increase the number of screening halls though, so maybe the soundproofing will be improved in the future. Admission is €5.50, except on Thursdays when it's a real bargain at €2.75. (Map area A7)

Biotoom 301 - Overtoom 301, 778-1145

http://squat.net/overtoom301

This 100-seat cinema is just one of the many cool projects going on at the Academie squat (see Party Venues, Music chapter). Films are shown a couple of days a week and the programming runs from classics to political documentaries to experimental films. To find the theatre, walk to the back of the building and up the stairs. Admission is just €2, or €3 for a double-bill. (Map area A7)

Tropeninstituut Theater - Linneausstraat 2, 568-8500

www.kit.nl/tropenmuseum

This theatre, attached to the Tropenmuseum, shows rarely-screened films from all around the world. They often compliment special exhibits at the museum, and are presented in a series - a month of comedies from Iran, for example. Call to find out if the subtitles are in English (they usually are). Admission: €5. (Map area H7)

film

The Movies - Haarlemmerdijk 161, 638-6016

www.themovies.nl

A mix of new mainstream and art films play in the four small halls that make up this theatre. They also have a popular late-night program on Friday and Saturday nights just after midnight. This is the oldest cinema that's still in use in Amsterdam and its little Art Deco lobby is beautiful, but at €7.50 the admission ain't cheap. (Map area C2)

De Munt - Vijzelstraat 16

Amsterdam's newest megaplex, De Munt - so named because it's right across the street from the pretty old mint building - has 13 halls showing the standard Hollywood fare. But they also offer a rep program of mostly English-language films every Monday night for only €4.50. And films shown before noon are only €4.50, too. It's modern, clean and comfortable. (Map area D6)

The City - Leidseplein, 623-4570

Totally mainstream, but the giant screen and excellent sound system in theatre #1 are great for movies like *Starship Troopers*. They offer a €4 deal on weekend mornings. Go to the Jamin candy store around the corner at Leidsestraat 98 to get your munchies before the film. (Map area C7)

easyCinema

www.easycinema.com

This huge orange conglomerate refused to give me any details about the cinema they plan to open here. But if it's such a big secret, how come they announced it on their website? If it's a good deal, I'll post the info on the *Get Lost!* site *(www.xs4all.nl/~getlost)*.

Fame Music - Kalverstraat 2, 638-2525

Okay, you're not really going to go here just to catch a flick. But if you do find yourself with some time to kill and you're near Dam Square, the basement of this record store has a big, flat-screen TV with surround sound and a couple of rows of movie theatre seats. Despite the bad house music drifting through, I sometimes enjoy ducking out of the rain and watching a bit of mainstream stuff like *Lord of the Rings* or *Spiderman*. Open: daily 10-19 (thurs 'til 21).

The Cabinet of Dr. Caligari

miscellaneous film stuff

Amnesty International Film Festival - 626-4436
www.amnesty.nl/filmfestival

The Amnesty International Film Festival is a five-day event focussing on human rights issues. Films and videos (fiction and documentary) are screened at the Balie and City (see above). To date there've been five of these festivals in Amsterdam. Check their website to see when the next one is scheduled.

International Documentary Film Festival (IDFA) - late November, 627-3329
www.idfa.nl

If you're in town at this time of year, look out for info on this famous festival. It's the biggest of its kind, with over 200 documentary films screened at several theatres around town. Special events include film-maker retrospectives, and programs like "Docs Around the Clock" - a whole night of films with breakfast served in the morning. Among other places, you can find the program at the AUB (see Music chapter), and De Balie (see above).

Shadow Documentary Film Festival - late November
www.shadowfestival.nl

This festival runs parallel to IDFA, but focusses more on experimental documentaries, often by unknown directors. Films are shown in the intimate setting of the Melkweg Cinema (see above) and the public is able to meet and talk with the film makers after each screening.

Roze Filmdagen (Pink Film Days) - December
www.rozefilmdagen.nl

In the past, themes at this annual gay and lesbian film fest have run from horror, to religion, to the "inevitable fate" of homosexual characters in movies. And of course there's always some porn. Though some of the program is culled from other, bigger queer festivals, it remains a somewhat underground event and a good opportunity to catch rarely-screened works. Films and videos are shown at The Cavia, Balie, and the Filmmuseum (see above).

Netherlands Film Museum Library - Vondelstraat 69-71, 589-1435
www.filmmuseum.nl

This library is a project of the Netherlands Film Museum (see above) and lies right at the edge of Vondelpark. It's a bright, airy space, that's perfect for browsing in if you're a film-lover. A large percentage of their 17,000 books are in English and there are over 1,700 magazines, too. You can't check books out, but there is a photocopier in the back. Stash your bags in the lockers by the entrance (you get your €.50 back when you leave). When you're finished, you might want to head up the street to the Manege Café (see Cafés chapter). Open: tues-fri 10-17; sat 11-17. (Map area A8)

De Filmcorner - Marnixstraat 263, 624-1974

This little shop is packed with used videos and films at good prices. Most of it's porno, but they've also got weird shit like super-8 Bruce Lee films and Jerry Lewis movies dubbed into German! Open: mon-fri 9-12 and 13-17:30; sat 9-16. (Map area B4)

film

The Silver Screen - Haarlemmerdijk 94, 638-1341

www.silverscreen.nl

New and used books and magazines all about film. Lots of good stuff to browse through here, including posters, cards, DVDs, videos, and laser discs. Other places to look for this kind of stuff are Cine-Qua-Non (Staalstraat 14; 625-5588) and, for posters, De Lach (1e Bloemdwarsstraat 14). The Silver Screen is open: mon-fri 13-18; sat 11-18. (Map area C2)

Ciné Ville - Spuistraat 232, 772-8461

www.cineville.0catch.com

Just in case you don't have your very own copy of *Shao Lin Soccer* yet, here's a cosy, split-level store that sells new and used DVDs and videos. They also stock posters, film-books, laserdisks, CDs and a good collection of soundtracks on vinyl. Open: mon-fri 14-20; sat/sun 12-18. (Map area C5)

Cult Videotheek - Amstel 47, 622-7843

www.cultvideo.nl

As a tourist, you probably won't end up here, but this is one of the coolest video and DVD rental outlets in Amsterdam. They have an impressive collection of over 5,000 videos including foreign films, sexploitation, cult and trash, anime, and a lot more. In the basement they sell second-hand videos and DVDs, too. Open: daily 13-22. (Map area E6)

Outdoor screening of The Harder They Come at Oosterpark.

Sex and lots of it: it's a big part of tourism in Amsterdam. The Red Light District is always crowded and colourful, not to mention sleazy. It's located in the neighbourhood just south-east of Central Station. You'll find streets and alleyways lined with sex shops, live sex the-atres, and rows and rows of red lights illuminating the windows of Amsterdam's famous prosti-tutes. This area is pretty safe, but women on their own sometimes get hassled and may want to tour this part of town during the day. Everyone should watch out for pickpockets.

There's also a smaller Red Light area around Spuistraat and the Singel Canal, near Central Station. And another, frequented mainly by Dutch men, runs along Ruysdaelkade by Albert Cuypstraat. But while the Red Light Districts are concentrated in these areas, several of the places I recommend below are in other parts of the city.

In case you were wondering, the services of a prostitute in the Red Light District start at €50 for a blow-job and €50 for a fuck. At that price you get about 15 to 20 minutes. The condom is included free of charge.

sex shops

You'll find them every twenty metres in the Red Light District and you should definitely take a peek inside one. These places all carry roughly the same selection of sex toys, magazines and videos, ranging from really funny to seriously sexy to disgusting. Remember that videos and DVDs play on different systems in different parts of the world. If you buy one, make sure to ask if it will play on your machine back home. The European system (except for France) is called PAL. North America uses NTSC. Also, most of the cheap stuff is of poor quality: you get what you pay for. For better quality goods I'd recommend the following shop...

Female and Partners - Spuistraat 100, 620-9152

www.femaleandpartners.nl

This is the coolest and classiest sex shop in Amsterdam. It's women-run and offers an alter-native to the very male-dominated sex industry. Inside you'll find a wide range of vibrators, dildos and other sex articles. They're always expanding their selection of books and movies, and they also have some incredibly sexy clothes that you won't find elsewhere. The pvc and latex wear is particularly impressive! Everything in the shop is also available via their very efficient mail-order service. Stop in for info on fetish parties as well. Open: sun/mon 13-18; tues-sat 11-18 (thurs 'til 21). (Map area C5)

Absolute Danny - Oudezijds Achterburgwal 78, 421-0915

www.absolutedanny.com

This fetish shop is also woman-run and you can tell the difference from other shops as soon as you walk in. It's much more stylish than the nearby sex stores here in the Red Light District. Single women and couples will feel comfortable shopping here. They stock sensual clothing for both men and women, Andrew Blake videos, and lots of S/M accessories. The owner, Danny, designs a lot of the clothes herself. Open: sat-wed 11-20; thurs/fri 11-21. (Map area E5)

Condomerie Het Gulden Vlies - Warmoesstraat 141, 627-4174

www.condomerie.com

This was the very first condomerie in the world - and what a selection! There's also an amusing display of condom boxes and wrappers. The laid-back atmosphere here makes the necessary task of buying and using condoms a lot of fun. Open: mon-sat 11-18. (Map area D4)

Nolly's Sexboetiek - Sarphatipark 99, 673-4757

In the back of this shop I found a bunch of dusty, straight and gay super 8 and 8mm films from the '60s and '70s for around €4 each. I don't have a projector, but collectors might be interested. Nolly also has a big selection of magazines, some that I didn't see in the Red Light District. Open: mon-fri 10-18; sat 10-17.

Blue and White - Ceintuurbaan 248, 610-1741

This is another sex shop that, like Nolly's, is in the neighbourhood of the Albert Cuyp Market (see Markets, Shopping chapter). They've been open for 30 years and they have all the required stuff plus a bargain bin full of dildos, other toys, and discount videos. Open: mon-fri 9:30-18 (thurs 'til 21); sat 12-17.

Miranda Sex Videotheek - Ceintuurbaan 354, 470-8130

Just down the road from Blue and White, this video store boasts that it stocks over 10,000 videos. Its two floors are loaded with more porn than you can shake a stick at. You'll find just about every kink and perversion you can imagine, and probably some that you can't. Open: daily 10-23.

Alpha Blue - Nieuwendijk 26, 627-1664

www.crusex.com

Apparently videos are cheaper here than in the nearby Red Light District, but I can't swear by it. They also stock a large selection of magazines. If you don't find what you're looking for, there are two more sex shops next door. Open: daily 9-1. (Map area D3)

The Bronx - Kerkstraat 53-55, 623-1548

www.bronx.nl

This sex shop for gay men has an impressive collection of books, magazines and videos. There are also leather goods, sex toys and the biggest butt-plug I've ever seen! There's a cinema in the back and some video cabins. If you get really worked up you can run across the street to "Thermos Night" (#58-60; 623-4936; *www.thermos.nl*; opens at 23:00), where €12.50 (€17.50 if you're under 24) gets you saunas, films, bars, and lots of sweaty guys. Bronx is open: daily 12-24. (Map area C6)

peep shows & live sex

There are several peep show places scattered around the Red Light District. There's one called Sexyland (St. Annendwarsstraat 4; Map area E4), and another called Sex Palace (Oudezijds Achterburgwal 84; Map area E5). I went into one and this is what I peeped. In a telephone-booth-sized room I put a two-euro coin in a slot and a little window went up. Lo and behold there was a young couple fucking on a revolving platform about a metre from my face. It wasn't very passionate, but they were definitely doing it. Two euros gets you about 90 seconds. Then I went into a little sit-down booth and for yet another two euros I got a couple of minutes of a video peep show. There is a built-in control panel with channel changer and a choice of over 150 videos. Everything is there, including bestiality and brown showers. The verdict? Well, I found it kind of interesting in a weird sort of way. There were mostly men peeping, obviously, but there were also some couples looking around. If you're curious, you should go take a look: nobody knows you here anyway.

penis fountain

In the name of research I also saw a few sex shows. At some you can bargain with the doorman, and the average admission price ends up being about €15. Inside an appropriately sleazy little theatre, women will strip to loud disco music. Sometimes they get someone from the audience to participate by removing lingerie or inserting a vibrator. Then a couple will have sex. It's very mechanical and not very exciting, but it will satisfy your curiosity. At other shows (like Casa Rosso; Oudezijds Achterburgwal 106; 627-8954; *www.casarosso.com*) you pay a set price of €25 to sit in a clean, comfortable theatre and watch better-looking strippers and couples. Again, it's not really sexy, but the show was more entertaining. I especially liked one couple who did a choreographed routine to Mozart's *Requiem*. It was very dramatic and the woman wore lots of leather and had several piercings!

miscellaneous sex stuff

Fetish Parties

Amsterdam is famous for it's fetish parties, where people can dance and socialize in an open manner, as well as enjoy the dungeons, darkrooms, and play areas provided. There's always a strict dress code, (leather, latex, etc). For a listing in English of all the parties around town, go online to Fetish Lights *(www.fetishlights.nl)*, or pick up flyers at Female and Partners (see above).

Prostitution Information Centre (PIC) - Enge Kerksteeg 3, 420-7328

www.pic-amsterdam.com

The PIC offers advice and information about prostitution in the Netherlands to tourists, prostitutes, their clients, and anyone else who's interested. It's located in the heart of the Red Light District and is open to the public. Inside you'll find pamphlets, flyers, and books about all aspects of prostitution. They also have a few souvenirs for sale. In the evenings they sometimes host lectures. Open: tues/wed/fri/sat 11:30-19:30 (possibly longer in the summer). (Map area E4)

Same Place - Nassaukade 120, 475-1981

www.sameplace.nl

There are lots of sex clubs in Amsterdam, but this one is unique because it bills itself as a "woman-friendly erotic dance café", and the cover charge isn't too expensive. Everyone is welcome: singles, couples, dykes, fags, fetishists, exhibitionists, transsexuals, and anyone else, but make sure you dress up. They have piercing and body-painting nights, kinky parties in their cellar (which has a dark-room and S/M corner), and sometimes women-only parties. Open: mon 21-1; tues-thurs 22-3; fri/sat 22-4. (Map area B4)

Amsterdam Call Girls - 600-2354

www.Amsterdam-Callgirls.com

This fully legal (registered at the chamber of commerce!) escort service is owned and co-operatively run by women. They've been in business for more than a decade and have an excellent reputation. If you have the money (it's very expensive), and go in for this sort of thing, this is who you should be supporting: women who have taken control of their chosen profession and, as a result, are making their lives and those of their colleagues healthier and safer. Couples are also welcome to call.

A Note About Prostitution

Because prostitution in the Netherlands has not been forced underground, it is one of the safest places in the world for sex-trade workers and their clients to do business. The status of prostitution in Holland was recently changed from "decriminalized" (subject to pragmatically suspended laws, as with soft drugs) to "legalized" (subject to the same laws as any business).

In spite of this progressive legal climate however, sex-trade workers remain socially stigmatised and are still often exploited. They're required to pay income tax, yet still report having difficultly opening bank accounts or arranging insurance policies if they're honest about the nature of their work. As a result, many of them continue to lead a double life and this is one of the reasons they have such a strong aversion to being photographed. (Don't do it: you're asking for trouble.)

Prostitutes in the Netherlands are not required by law to undergo STD testing. This situation is strongly supported by the prostitutes union (The Red Thread) and members of the women's movement who work to ensure the human rights of sex-trade workers.

Note: "g" is pronounced like a low growl, like the noise you make when you try to scratch an itch at the back of your throat, like the ch in Chanukah. I'll use "gh" in my attempt at the phonetic spellings. Good luck (you'll need it).

hello / goodbye	= dag (dagh)
see ya	= tot ziens (tote zeens)
thank you	= dank je wel / bedankt (dahnk ye vel / bidahnkt)
you're welcome / please	= alsjeblieft (allsh-yuhbleeft)
fuck off	= rot op
do you speak english?	= spreekt uw engels? (spreykt oo angles)
how much does that cost?	= hoe veel kost dat? (hoo feyl cost dat)
free	= gratis (ghrah-tis)
stoned as a shrimp	= stoned als een garnaal
got a light?	= vuurtje? (foortchye)
rolling paper	= vloeitje (flu-ee-chye)
to smoke grass	= blow
to blowjob	= pijpen (pie-pen)
store	= winkel (veenkel)
delicious	= lekker
food, to eat, meal	= eten (ayten)
rice / noodles	= nasi / bami (in Indonesian restaurants)

bon apetit	= eet smakelijk (ate sma-ke-lik)
dessert	= toetje (too-chye)
cosy	= gezellig (ghezeligh)
really?	= echt waar? (eght var)
what a drag	= wat jammer (vhat yahmmer)
juice	= sap
cheers	= proost
watch out	= pas op
squat	= kraak (krahk)
fag	= nicht (nickte)
dykes	= potten
bicycle	= fiets (feets)
left	= links (leenks)
right	= rechts
asshole!	= klootzak! (literally "scrotum" or "ball-bag"; kloat-zak)
I practice safe sex	= Ik vrij veilig (Ik fry file-igh)

dictionary continued...

1 = een (eyn)	**1 ounce** = 28 grams	**Time:**
2 = twee (tvey)	**1 kilo** = 2.2 pounds	
3 = drie (dree)		**12 noon** 12:00
4 = vier (feer)	**Temperatures:**	**1 pm** 13:00
5 = vijf (fife)	**°F °C**	**2 pm** 14:00
6 = zes (zes)	104 = 40	**3 pm** 15:00
7 = zeven (zeven)	95 = 35	**4 pm** 16:00
8 = acht (ahcht)	86 = 30	**5 pm** 17:00
9 = negen (nayghen)	77 = 25	**6 pm** 18:00
10 = tien (teen)	68 = 20	**7 pm** 19:00
	59 = 15	**8 pm** 20:00
	50 = 10	**9 pm** 21:00
Days:	41 = 5	**10 pm** 22:00
	32 = 0	**11 pm** 23:00
mon = ma (maandag)	23 = -5	**12 midnight** 00:00
tues = di (dinsdag)	14 = -10	**1 am** 01:00
wed = wo (woensdag)	5 = -15	**2 am** 02:00
thurs = do (donderdag)	-4 = -20	**3 am** 03:00
fri = vri (vrijdag)	-13 = -25	etc..
sat = za (zaterdag)		
sun = zo (zondag)	**cold** = koud (cowd)	**what time is it?** = hoe laat
	hot = heet (hate)	is het (who laht is het)
	rain = regen (ray-ghen)	

emergency & health

Emergency: (police, ambulance, fire) 112

Police: (non-emergency) 0900-8844

First Aid: (OLVG Hospital, 1st Oosterparkstraat 179) 599-9111

Sexual Assault Help Line: (mon-fri 10:30-23:00; sat/sun 16-23:00) 613-0245

Crisis Help Line: (24 hours; if you get a message, they're talking with someone else who's in crisis) 675-7575 or 0900-0767

Anti-Discrimination Office: (complaints about fascism and racism; mon-fri 9-17:00) 638-5551

Doctor Referral Service: (24 hours) 592-3388 or 592-3434

Women's Health Centre: (free advice and referrals, but no in-house docs; Vrouwengezondheidscentrum Isis, Obiplein 14; mon-fri 10-13:00) 693-4358

Travellers' Vaccination Clinic: (GG & GD, Nieuwe Achtergracht 100; mon-fri 7:30-10:00) 555-5370

Dentist Referral Service: (24 hours) 570-9595

ACTA Dental Clinic: (cheap treatment by students; mon-fri 9-17:00) 518-8888

Pharmacies Info Line: (includes after-hours locations; message is in Dutch) 694-8709

Aids Info Line: (anonymous consultation about aids and safe sex; mon-fri 14-22:00; sat/sun 24 hours) 0900-204-2040

STD Clinic: (free and anonymous treatment; GG&GD, Groenburgwal 44; mon-fri 9-12:30, 13:30-17:30) 555-5822

Birth Control Clinic: (Rutgershuis, Sarphatistraat 618; mon-fri 9-16:00) 616-6222

Abortion & Birth Control Info Line: (mon-fri 9-22:00) 0900-1450

Legal Aid Clinic: (mon-fri 14-17:00) 520-5100

general info lines

Dutch Directory Assistance: (€.90/call) 0900-8008

International Directory Assistance: (€1.15/call) 0900-8418

Collect Calls: 0800-0410

Amsterdam Tourist Office (VVV): (€.55/min, which adds up quickly as they often leave you on hold for ages; mon-fri 9-17:00) 0900-400-4040

Public Transport Info: (info on trains, buses & trams throughout Holland; €.50/min) 0900-9292

International Train Info & Reservations: (€.25/min) 0900-9296

Taxi: 677-7777

Schiphol Airport: (€.10/min) 0900-0141

Lost and Found Offices: Amsterdam Police (Stephenstraat 18, near Amstel Station; mon-fri 12-15:30) 559-3005; Central Station (mon-fri 8-20:00; sat 9-17:00) 030-235-3923; Public Transit Authority (mon-fri 9-16:30) 460-5858

Lost Credit Cards: (all open 24 hours) Amex 504-8666; Mastercard/Eurocard 030-283-5555; Visa 660-0611; Diners 654-5511

Gay and Lesbian Switchboard: (info and advice; daily 14-22:00; *www.switchboard.nl*) 623-6565

Youth Advice Centre: (tues-fri 13-17:00; thurs 13-20:00) 344-6300

Women's Centre: (Vrouwenhuis Amsterdam, Nieuwe Herengracht 95; café - with free e-mail access! - open wed/thurs 12-17:00; *www.vrouwenhuis.nl*) 625-2066

Weather Forecast: (recorded message in Dutch; €.50/min) 0900-8003

embassies & consulates

(070 = Den Haag)

Amerika 575-5309 / 070-310-9209

Australia 070-310-8200

Austria 471-2438 / 070-324-5470

Belgium 070-312-3456

Britain 676-4343 / 070-364-5800

Canada 070-311-1600

Denmark 070-302-5959

Egypt 070-354-2000

Finland 070-346-9754

France 530-6969 / 070-312-5800

Germany 673-6245 / 070-342-0600

Greece 070-363-8700

Hungary 070-350-0404

Indonesia 070-310-8100

India 070-346-9771

Ireland 070-363-0993

Israel 070-376-0500

Italy 550-2050 / 070-346-9249

Japan 070-346-9544

Luxembourg 070-360-7516

Morocco 070-346-9617

New Zealand/Aotearoa 070-346-9324

Norway 624-2331 / 070-311-7611

Poland 070-360-2806

Portugal 070-363-0217

Russia 070-364-6473

South Africa 070-392-4501

Spain 620-3811 / 070-364-3814

Surinam 070-365-0844

Sweden 070-412-0200

Switzerland 664-4231 / 070-364-2831

Thailand 465-1532 / 070-345-2088